I was asked to write something about art in the West today, to offer some insights on how art functions in an increasingly pluralistic and fractured society, at a time when no dominant artistic movement guides us, in a part of the country that has no greater tradition than its desire to periodically reinvent itself. The danger is clear, for too often this kind of regional boosterism gets caught in the awkward position of justifying any well-intentioned endeavor within its borders. Generalities abound, and anything specific implicitly denies what's left out. And yet, as a born and raised westerner, I believe there are qualities we share in different proportions than human beings in other areas of the country. What follows is a meandering series of personal reflections, a fragmented, private history in the West written, if you will, in the gaps of stories not told.

I think we have to get beyond the scenic West to arrive at any original, quality notions about the art made here. Teddy Roosevelt called the stretch of highway from Yellowstone to Cody the most scenic fifty-two miles of road in America. He probably didn't mean that as an absolute, but it got printed, and you can see why he said it, even though there are plenty of other roads that are equally picturesque: the North Cascades highway, for instance, or coming into Bryce through Red Canyon or crossing the Continental Divide west of Taos. But such places are exceptions to the rule. When I think of the West—"the real West"—I think of places that have permanent vacancy signs by the road. You know, a place where tumbleweed might actually drift by—or at least an old, crusty Burger King wrapper; where one of those scrawny, sun-blistered people might step out and surprise you; someplace like Beatty, Nevada, or Manderson, Wyoming.

Here's one difference between being an artist in the West and the East: In the West, you never know just where your influences are going to come from. Part of this is due to the pervasive role of the road. Think of all those movies, from *Easy Rider* to *Thelma & Louise*. Roads and borders. Roads and borders. Western states are as big as most countries, so crossing their borders actually counts for some sort of passage. I mean: Delaware? Connecticut? We have *days* between one state and another.

In the East, artists may find out where they fit into the culture by going to museums. In the West, you drive. On the road, confluences come by chance. You can be driving in the middle of nowhere, and if there's a narrow bridge, another car or truck will surely come up from the other side simultaneous to your own crossing. In the West, you find love and friendship this same way since time and life's myths are opened up by all the distance between. Notions of nearness become loaded with relativity in the context of such expanse: face-to-face, earth to sky, neighborliness, remoteness, magnitude. Your nearest neighbor could be miles away, thus "closeness" depends little on actual distance.[1] Compound that by the fact that in between you never know what's going to happen. People control what they can, but the West is not a stable place. This is partly what is meant by living in the atmosphere of destiny.

The road also means we have a line on time and space. "Wall Drug, 610 miles." In the West, you can pretty much calculate those miles into time: 610 divided by 60 mph equals 10 hours give or take 10 or 15 minutes to Wall Drug, the edge of the West. You don't have to go there to be aware of it. You don't have to be anywhere near it to pass a sign that makes you think maybe you should go. It's another one of those instances of being where you are and somewhere else at the same time. Driving, you get in this zone where the hum of the tires and wind combines with the view through your sunglasses to the window, and specific images have the time to be properly pondered. Tuned in, you see them coming, beginning the rumination before you even know what they might be.

Roads constitute what culture is in the West, and art influences can be anything that is built near them, especially in contrast to all that is not. Call it the unpredictable provocation of the West's inherent minimalism, but most of it is stuff that has cropped up alongside roads, particularly in the last fifty years, as recent incursions into the realm of geologic time: the rich and improbable carving out of the desert into a quarter-acre junkyard; a rock with "I, Zoilo, love Kimberly" painted on it; slanting, skeletal remains of barns or shacks or a closed-up stand for selling Zuni jewelry.

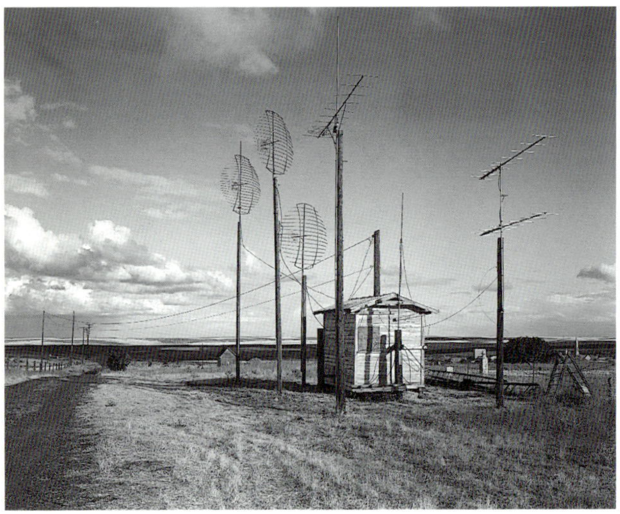

MICHAEL BURNS
81 - 154 NEAR GRASS VALLEY, OREGON, *1981*
Contact gelatin silver print, 8″ × 10″

Dave Hickey, a lifelong westerner, may have said it best when he described the West *as a place where things break down and don't get fixed, and people do too—where the relationship between nature and culture is so self-evidently and radically dysfunctional that you can hardly imagine it otherwise.*[2] Henry Nash Smith said the same thing in what must have been a bid for best Victorian prose written in 1950: *The capital difficulty of the American agrarian tradition is that it accepted the paired but contradictory ideas of nature and culture as a general principle of historical and social interpretation.*[3] In other words, despite Frank Lloyd Wright, we have never been able to figure out the principles of contextuality. This dysfunctionality is our strength, our embarrassment, our success and failure.

The willingness to live with contradictions between nature and culture is how Sam Smith, a Northwest turn-of-the-century railroad man, could look out on the Columbia River Gorge and reimagine it as a ribbon of lavish castles, a veritable new Rhine. He not only built Maryhill Mansion on a glorious cliff overlooking the river near Goldendale, Washington in 1914, but went on to further confuse his cultural and historical dreams by building a concrete replica of Stonehenge about three miles away, as a monument to the World War I dead. (Smith had heard that the Druids used the original for human sacrifice and felt that war was the ultimate human sacrifice.) Maryhill is now a lovely, eccentric, isolated anomaly of a museum and Smith's Stonehenge, a dusty site in mild neglect.

Such willful distortions of reality allowed D. W. Griffith to re-create the Great Wall of Babylon in Hollywood, in 1916, for his epic movie *Intolerance*, at the cost of half a million dollars, enough to make forty features of that day at their average cost of $12,500. The movie and the set itself "proved that a movie's capacity to create a world was virtually limitless."[4] Now the site of the Hollywood Safeway, the wall loomed over Vermont and Sunset before it was finally torn down in the 1920s. It set a precedent for everything from the wild, seemingly endless cross-fertilization between Disneyland and Las Vegas to the outrageous decision to place London Bridge on the Colorado River at Lake Havasu. You get so used to the non-sense that logic becomes nothing more than extra baggage. A billboard displaying rolling green lawns, lakes, and trees stuck by the side of a desolate desert road begins to look like a perfectly fine idea. The weird functionality of the giant steel umbrella over Casa Grande Ruins near Coolidge, Arizona, does too. I mean, it can get *hot* in Arizona!

What makes all these things work is the righteous fact that they exist completely out of context. They are self-defining and have come into being through the sheer will of their creators. Obviously, like art.

The first artist I ever knew personally was an old guy named Spaceman in Ocean Beach, California, in 1968. When he was drying out, he stayed with our neighbor, Mr. Oaks, at his cottage by the pier. Spaceman "painted with light," black-light paintings of a planet called Relisborg that he'd visited on three separate occasions. The first time he made the big leap into the spaceship he had been on a prison work crew out in the Mojave. From then on, he would go back and wander around in the desert for days and nights at a time, placing himself in the way of opportunity—or accessing artistic inspiration, according to your own interpretation of his quest. All you can say for certain is that he must have seen an unbelievable number of stars, staring out into the night sky that way.

I can't really tell you if his paintings were exceptional by any standards by which I've since learned to understand paintings. He had two distinct styles: one, a precise architectural surrealism, fairly classic sci-fi stuff; the other, a totally abstract drip method like Jackson Pollock's. Not knowing who Jackson Pollock was helped us all appreciate Spaceman's work on its own terms, but the black light and the chemical ambience really put whatever special gifts the paintings inherently offered over the top. And Spaceman's stories—you know, there's nothing like a good docent tour to make art convincing. He described huge ships the size of cities where the atmosphere was one of "total, unqualified, and abiding love." He gave us all "space numbers" that we were to use on the day the world ended when the Relisborgians would pick us up. He believed art was one of the healing forces in the universe. Sound familiar? I said the *universe*, and we had numbers with first priority. Knowing your primary audience is important. But the main thing with Spaceman, as with any other artist, was not whether he really went there but that he took us there.

Despite the intergalactic connections of someone like Spaceman, the West used to be more isolated than it is today. Isolated geographically and also in terms of historical perspective: If Europe saw all of America as culturally deficient, those poor souls on the right-hand side of the North American continent saw those of us in the West as a combination of depraved and deranged. We'll choose to look at this positively and say that it kept our defenses up and protected our individuality. This is less true today, but it is worth remembering that some of the most dynamic art of the last quarter century—and some of the most effective attacks on the canons of modernism—came from western artists before so many institutions expanded their ambitions, before the presence of regional gallery scenes, and before the art schools got so hip.

You produce a different kind of art if you don't encounter its paradigms very often. Like art nobody thought of before. Like Ed Kienholz's and Ed Ruscha's, the yin and yang of insight into western popular culture of the 1960s, before Los Angeles was anything but a cultural backwater. Like Judy Chicago's and Suzanne Lacey's and the women who turned a building into The Woman's Building giving feminist art its first real jump-start. Like Bruce Nauman in San Francisco, John Baldessari in San Diego, and Robert Irwin in West L.A. Like the absolute macho presumption of going out into the desert and creating not mere artworks but *earth* works. Like what Chris Burden said: "Art is a free spot in society, where you can do anything." And a whole series of ideas about what art could be, largely emanating from the pages of what may very well be the single most important art institution to come out of the West, *Artforum* magazine. (Sorry, but you have to take the bad with the good. Hey, blame what you don't like on the fact that it moved to New York.)

But I'm supposed to say something about being an artist in the West *today*. I gotta tell you, I don't have a good answer. I have only those fragmentary thoughts that have nothing in common but the gap between the great western tradition of eccentric visionary ideals and "real life."

I keep coming back to this: I watched the television coverage of the first night of the L.A. riots from a hotel room in Flagstaff, Arizona. I hold this thought like an old scrap of paper, unable to discard it. I was there visiting Jim and Julia Turrell, and we had been to the crater that day, the glorious *Roden Crater*, which is, depending on how you look at it, either the last great gasp of male ego manipulation of mother earth or, as my experience leads me to believe, potentially the most wonderful work of art created since, say, the Italian Renaissance. Pretentious? Yes. Essential? Yes. As it is, as a site, it is hard to beat, and its lightly excavated, replanted bowl allows for the sky to cup over you as a luminous, sensuous membrane of colored light. The scale of the crater is more stadiumlike than mountainlike, and it acts as a place of human refuge from the vast, inhuman, high desert country around it, and by offering refuge, connects you to the cosmos within view. Being there, you don't want to leave. You want all things to connect to the cosmos all the time.[5]

Back in town, I turned on the TV to relax before dinner, and the unfathomable Rodney King verdict had just come in. I spent the rest of the night hooked to a 24-hour news channel satellite feed from L.A., watching my home city erupt in flames and chaos and fear. Jean Baudrillard said, "There is nothing to match flying over Los Angeles by night."[6] He was right when he said it, when L.A. was convincingly portrayed as all things future. But he did not have that night's picture imposed on the megalopolis, as the vast constellations of fires and lights turned into our culture's most abiding vision of what the apocalypse should look like. L.A. finally became the place not where dreams can be fulfilled but where many end.

Where does this leave us today? Aside from Los Angeles probably being less of a magnet than it once was, we seem to be entering a sort of Borgesian notion of a world of not one center but many centers, where everywhere is center. Start with the fact that the state of Nevada is delineated at each intersection of highway and state line with neon that competes with the sunset and proclaims, "Last Chance." That means all chances are within. This also means an ever-increasing pluralism, which puts more complex demands not only on the artist but also on the audience—and the agencies like WESTAF who serve as crossing guards between the two.

Mike Kelley recently said, "Increasingly art is separated from the modernist model: Instead of revealing essentials, it's about revealing contradictions."[7] This is not endemic solely to this region, but we deal with contradictions in the West more directly because we still live within the myth—or afterglow—of its promises. If we concentrate on the gap instead of the failure or the promise, if we suspend some judgment and concentrate on the line where the cup is half full *and* half empty, we take on an open attitude that is akin to a state between childhood and adulthood, before acquiescence, between not knowing and acceptance, before reconciliation. This gap between promise and reality is one of the enduring themes in the West. It's an adolescent thing that comes out of knowing the reality does not match up with the promise—but not being quite sure *how* it doesn't. It is a state that is capable of being entirely fascinated by its own confusion and its own anxiety. Indeed, teenage life in America is largely a natural proclivity for expanding the range of contradictions, which is interpreted by most adults as a form of obnoxiousness.

This ability to juggle and expand the range of contradictions is also one of the fundamental assumptions of contemporary art practices, which of course is interpreted by most adults as. . .obnoxious. In many ways, balance in contemporary art is tension: an ability to be provocative in a seductive way. We refer to it as "extending the paradigms of art," but we really mean developing higher tolerances for what is outrageous. The point is to acknowledge and hold the extremes, and the art is the glue that keeps the contradictions together.

All artists must occasionally feel like the chief car repossessor, played by Harry Dean Stanton, in the movie *Repo Man*: *Look at those assholes over there. Ordinary fuckin' people. I hate 'em. See, an ordinary person spends his life* avoiding *tense situations. Repo Man spends his life* getting *into tense situations.*[8] We might all feel that way at times, but perhaps we should say our job in the arts is to encourage people to think they are not ordinary, that they can handle several extreme and conflicting ideas at the same time. Somebody has to do it.

An artistic equivalent of *Repo Man* was Survival Research Laboratories (SRL) from San Francisco, art that would certainly be classified under the "New Genres" category.[9] Anyone who ever witnessed an SRL performance will likely never forget the chaos, violent noise, and destructive capacity of the monstrous, handmade, remote-controlled, subject-to-malfunction machines. Art historians would of course drag out the precedent of Jean Tinguely, but SRL was more of an excessive exercise in bad attitude, kind of Jackson Pollock with weapons. The performances were so loud you literally could not hear yourself think, let alone wonder whether it was art or not.

I come across quite a number of artists in the West who in one way or another speak in terms of the viewer not needing any context or prior knowledge to appreciate their art. This is not simply some contemporary spin on pop art or postmodernist cultural pastiche. What many of these artists mean when they distinguish their work from a reliance on the prescribed canons of art has to do with a desire to connect with a more accessible, universal human experience rather than a culturally ordained concept. It is at heart a classic case of western populism that calls into account uppity, "high" art systems on behalf of an interested general audience. One might ask what the good news is when you loosen the ties to art history, but it begins to explain the need for the New Genres category. In this way, New Genres is not a question of media but rather a term that implies *no* genre or *any* genre. Such work enters into the creative process armed with the anxiety of unlimited freedom, with no refuge but intentionality.

Here we may recall the resolutely independent intentionality of everyone from Sam Smith and Spaceman to Jim Turrell. But intentionality may now also imply an increased interest in connecting with audience, and we see this manifested in various ways by the WESTAF fellowship artists. The social fabric, our "culture of contradictions," is often acknowledged with great specificity. Refreshingly, there is virtually no work that lobbies the generalities of hard political constructs, nor is there work that relies on the blanket of mass media but rather an interest in the more subtle vagaries of human existence, most generally from a determinedly personal point of reference.

I am impressed by the way so many of these artists have related to the "outside" histories of the region, such as Trimpin, who simultaneously draws inspiration and brings new life from the great hobo musician/inventor Harry Partch, or Susan Kelk Cervantes, who continues the fabulous Chicano mural work of such artists as Judy Baca and East Los Streetscapers. We see work by artists who draw on their immediate environments—reflective selves in community—like Sandow Birk, who has collaborated with neighborhood graffiti artists, or like James L. Acord, who has availed himself of the materials and technologies of his local nuclear reservation, or Cinthea Fiss, who tells of her own experience as a blue-collar worker in male-dominated trades. The uniqueness of each expression is underscored by Susan Magnus' elegant, minimalist images of keys, which read as perfect symbols of the privacy of poetic possession.

I've wanted to use a particular line by Richard Ford since I've first read it, and I think that it applies here: "I am looking for stories that will be axes for the frozen sea within us."[10] It seems to me that now—after more than a century of dealing with form and a couple decades of wrestling with how we might return to meaningful content, and then finding factionalist political and social issues only occasionally interesting—one of our options is to return to the western tradition of discovering and working out our own stories, of digging deep to excavate our own personal metaphors, if you will, in order to reconnect with the complicated swirl of life. All this suggests the potential of a new definition of regionalism—one that is informed by a global concern and consciousness but does not take the international media's vision of art as the defining paradigm. This is work that accesses the available imagery and life within the artist's reach, a reach that seeks centers of vulnerability rather than a center of power, a reach that seeks to touch the interior sparks of humanity.

It is precisely here that I applaud the WESTAF process and its mission, because the organization has chosen to acknowledge the private artistic act and to concentrate on individual expression even amid the clamor for a public institution to provide a public justification for art. The art and artists WESTAF has encouraged exemplify the possibilities for inhabiting centers with no dominant center, for exploring the pain and beauty of being in that uncertain state of grace where one is open to contradictions, and from which one may express what it's like to live in the space between promise and reality.

NOTES

1. From Gary Hill's video installation *Between Cinema and a Hard Place* (1991), the spoken text of which is taken from *The Nature of Language* by Martin Heidegger.

2. Dave Hickey, "The Code of the West," *Vernon Fisher* (La Jolla Museum of Contemporary Art, 1989), p. 22.

3. Henry Nash Smith, *Virgin Land: The American West as Symbol and Myth* (New York: Vintage Books, 1950), p. 305.

4. Michael Ventura, *Shadow Dancing in the U.S.A.* (Los Angeles: Jeremy P. Tarcher, Inc., 1985), p. 163.

5. Parenthetically here I want to note how intimate the relationship between place and human body is at *Roden Crater.* We get used to seeing aerial photographs of places like this (and *Double Negative* in Nevada, the *Spiral Jetty* in Utah, and *The Lightning Field* in New Mexico), and they seem such prominent incursions into nature. These pictures tell us as much about the frame of the camera as anything else, and its ability to isolate and dramatize a site. In actuality, the crater is a place to be in and look from, not a monumental sculpture to look at.

6. David Reid, *Sex, Death, and God in L.A.* (New York: Random House, Inc., 1992), p. xiii.

7. Robert Storr, "An Interview with Mike Kelley," *Art in America* (New York, vol. 82, no. 6, June 1994), p. 92.

8. Michael Nesmith, Producer, and Alex Cox, Director, *Repo Man* (Universal City, Universal Studios, 1984).

9. Survival Research member Matt Heckert was awarded a WESTAF fellowship for sculpture in 1991.

10. Richard Ford and Shannon Ravenel, eds., *The Best American Short Stories 1990* (Boston: Houghton Mifflin Company, 1990), p. xvii.

IMAGES

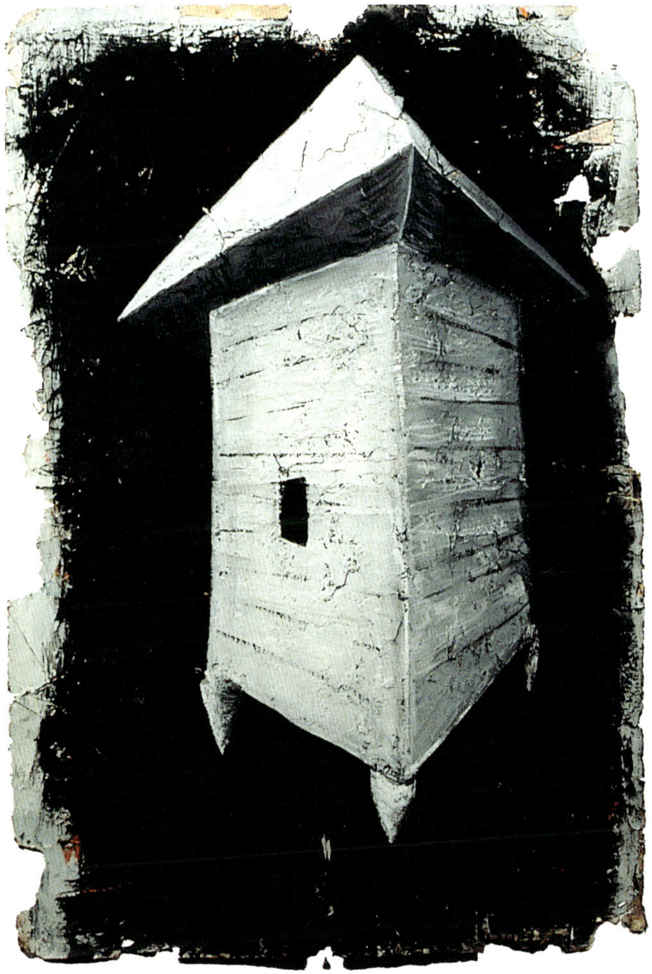

FAN WARREN
Empire of a Darker People, 1991
Mixed media, 43½″ × 29″
Collection of Erskine Peters

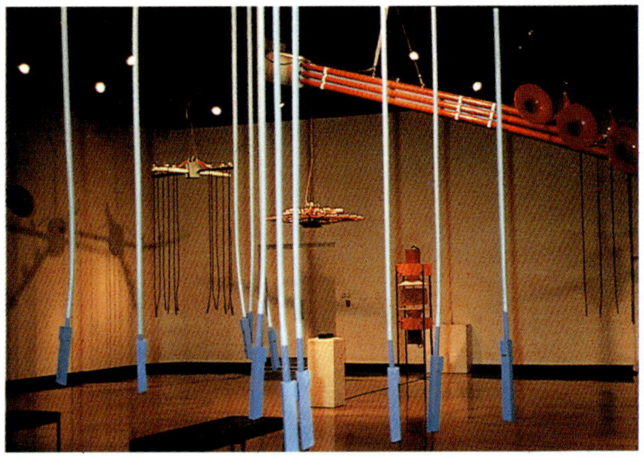

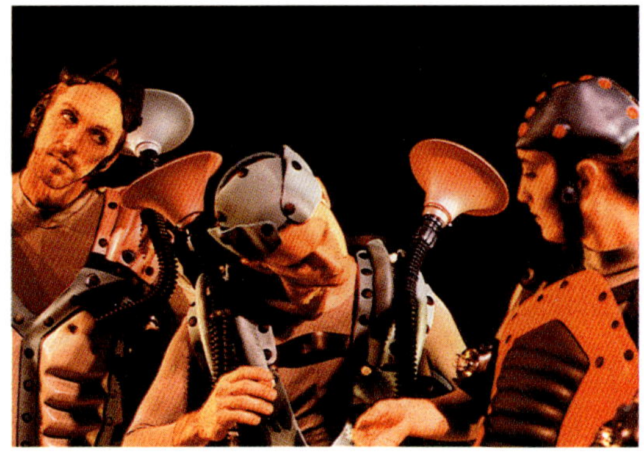

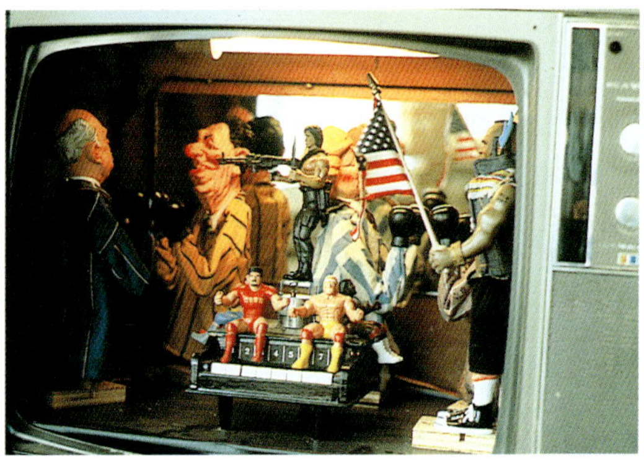

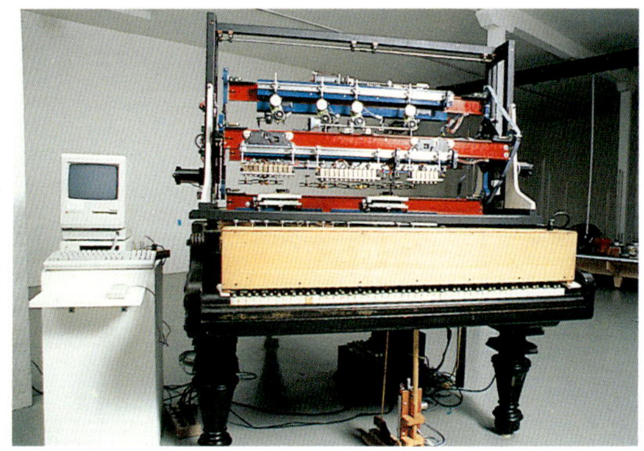

TRIMPIN
Clockwise from top left:
Phffft-Arrrgh, 1992
Interactive music sculpture, 20′ × 40′ × 70′
D.R.A.M.A. Ohno, 1993 Performance
Contraption IPP, 1992 Performance
and installation, 2′ × 3′ × 4′
TV Soap, 1991
Interactive sculpture, 3′ × 2′ × 2′

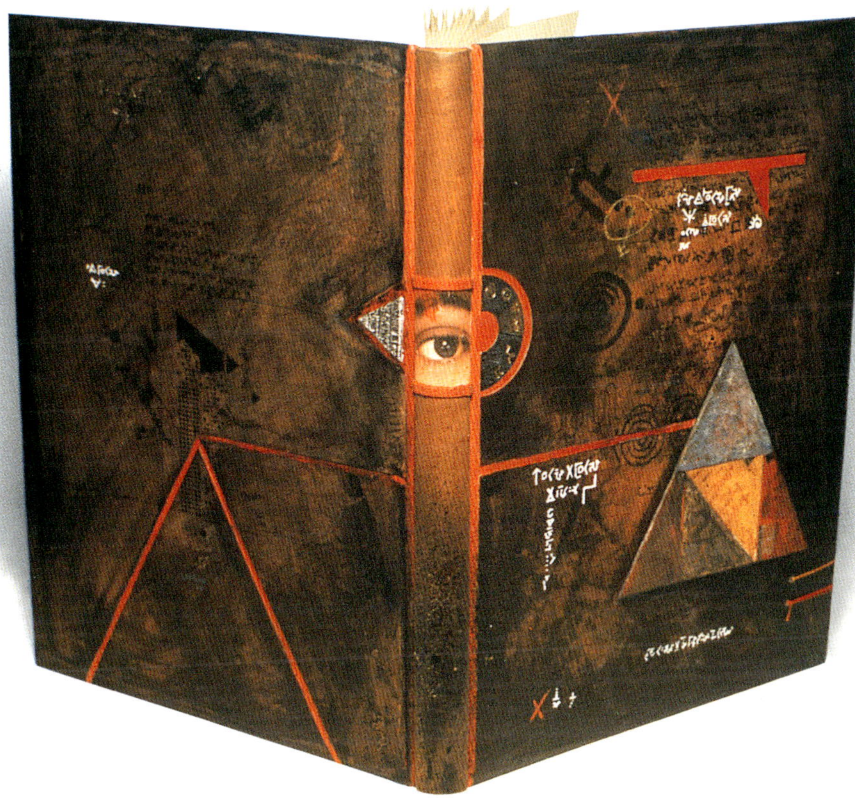

TIMOTHY C. ELY
On Psychometry, 1990
Leather, paper, metals, resins, pigment, silk, 12½" × 7⅜"
Collection of Rijksmuseum Meermanno-Westreenianum, Den Haag, The Netherlands

He was a smart boy, quick to pick things up, *very* industrious, but you've got to take risks in this business, you've got to go out on a limb sometimes, and, uh, he just didn't have the heart for it.
(Recording activated and heard when viewer touches heart, Digital Museum, *1993)*

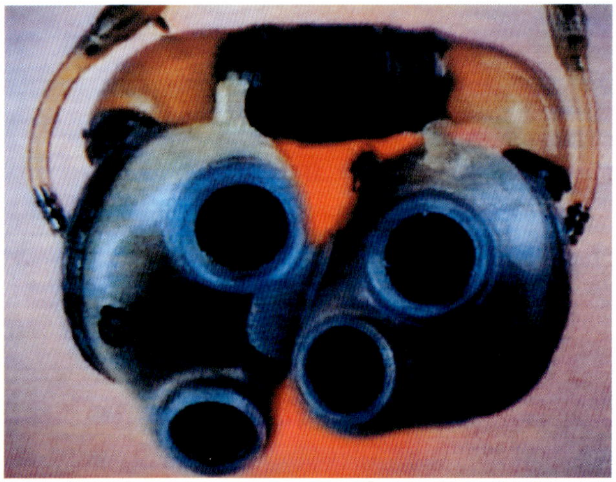

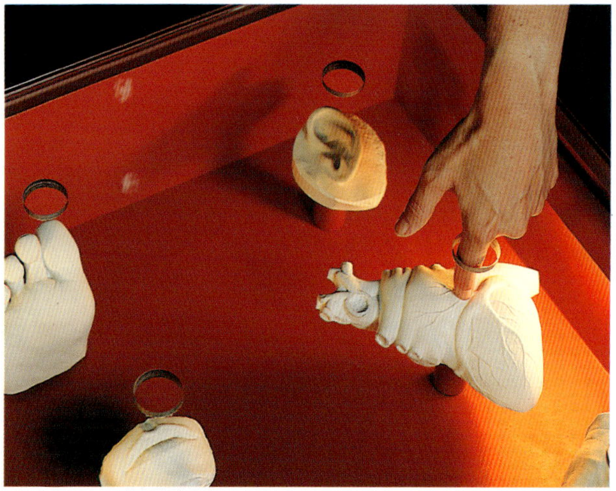

SARA ROBERTS
Digital Museum, 1993
Mixed/electronic media,
4 pieces, 36″ × 36″ × 32″ each

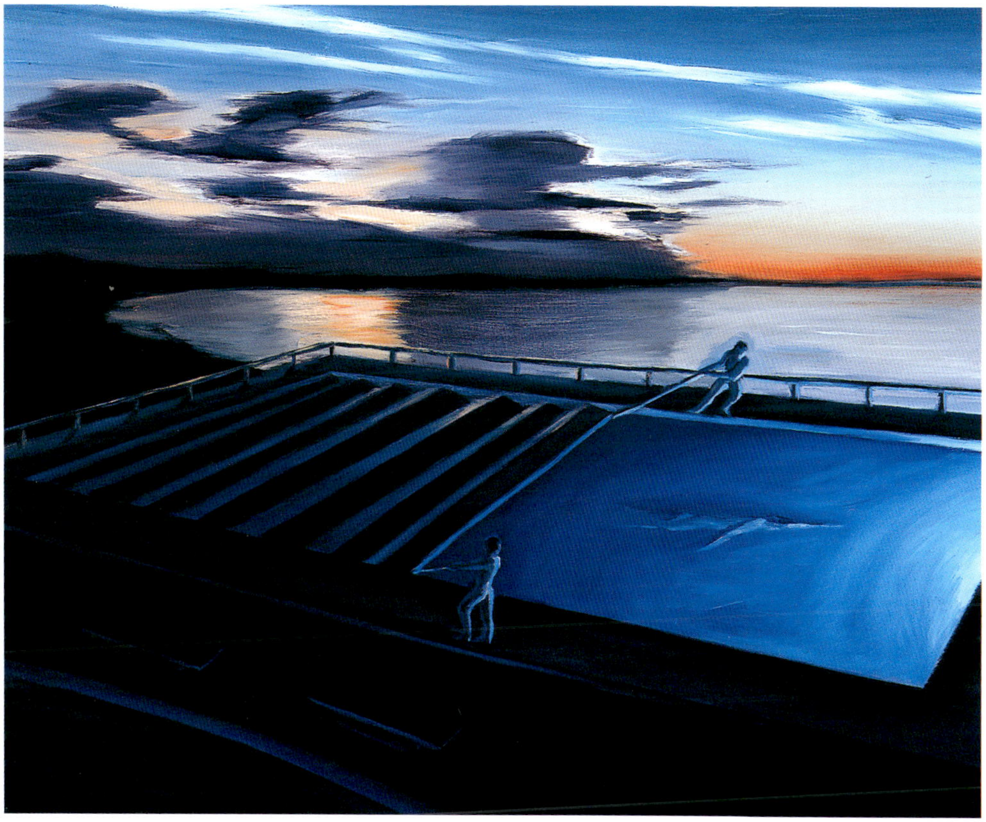

DENNIS L. ANGEL
The Pool Cover, 1993
Oil on panel, 32″ × 40″

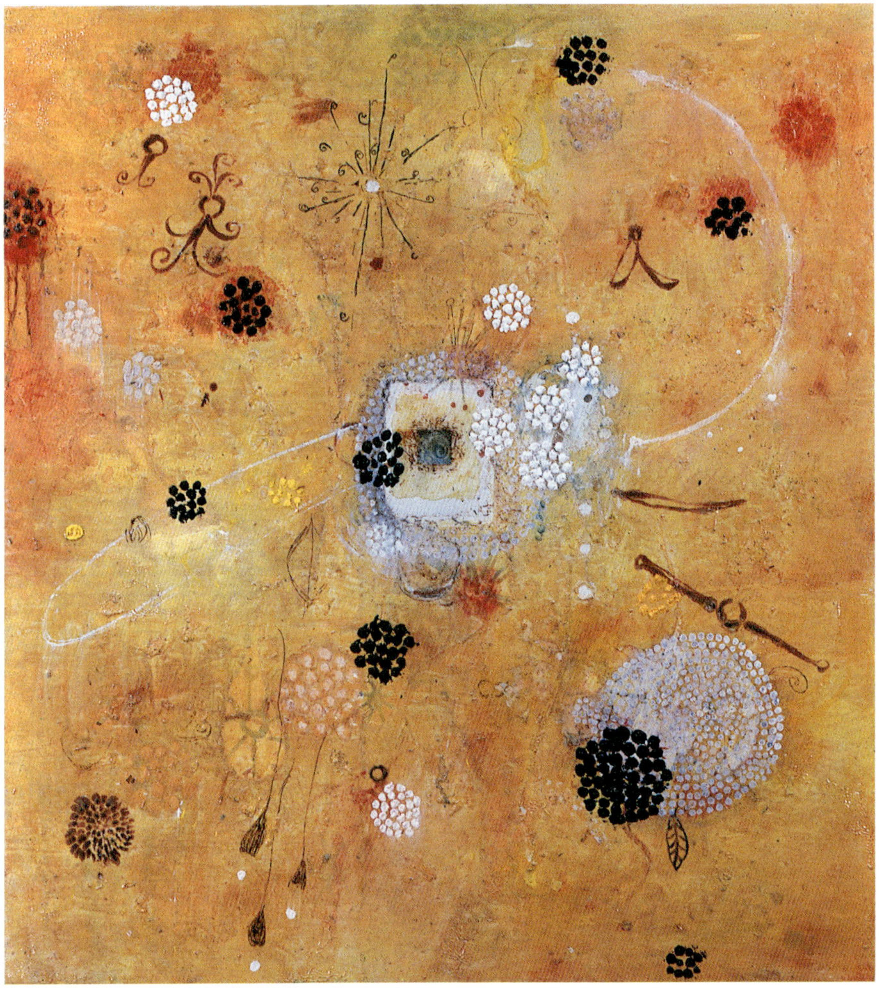

MAURA BENDETT
Blue Spiral and Grape Clusters, 1994
Oil, ballpoint pen, saffron,
etching, resin on canvas,
39" × 36" × 1¾"

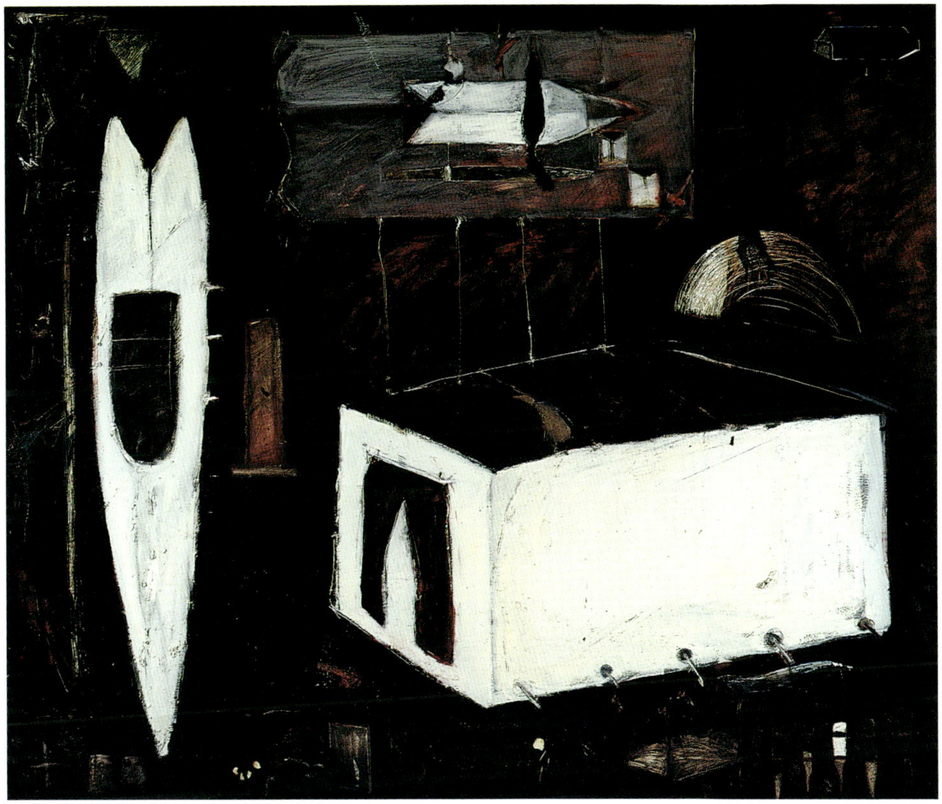

DOROTHY A. FAISON
Ritual Protection, 1990–93
Oil, charcoal, dog hair on canvas,
75″ × 84″, Collection of
Honolulu Academy of Arts

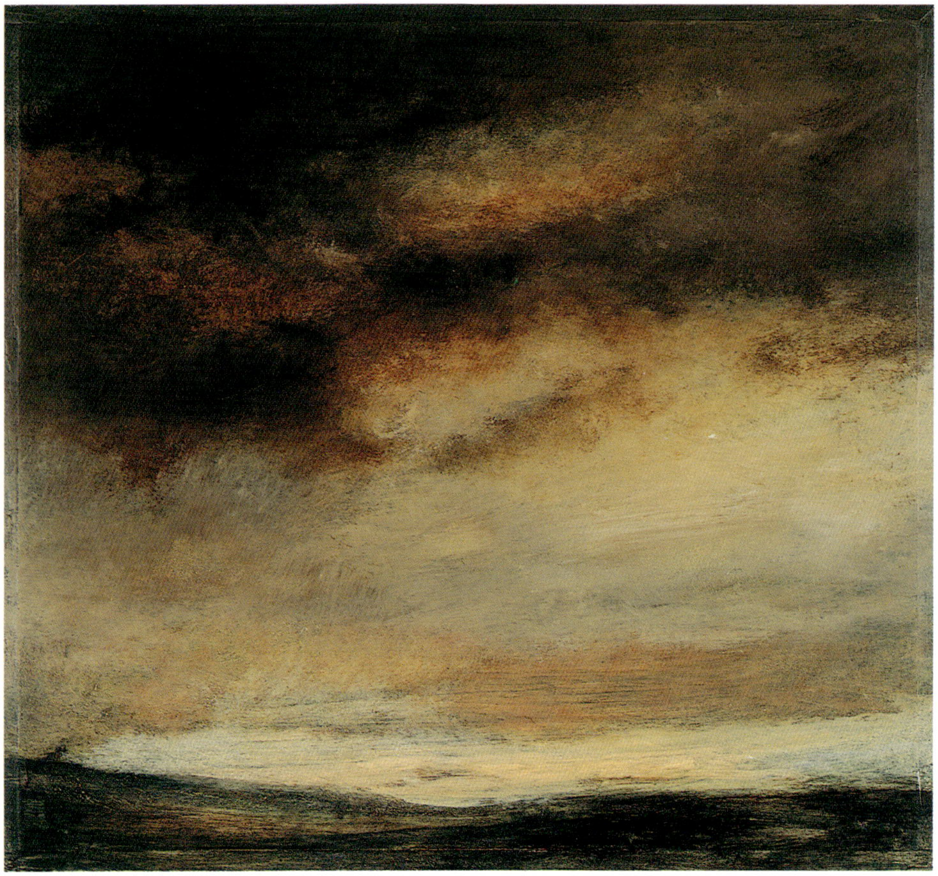

KAY FRENCH
Blow, 1993
Acrylic on wood, 18″ × 20″
Courtesy of Alex Paul and
Laura Ross-Paul

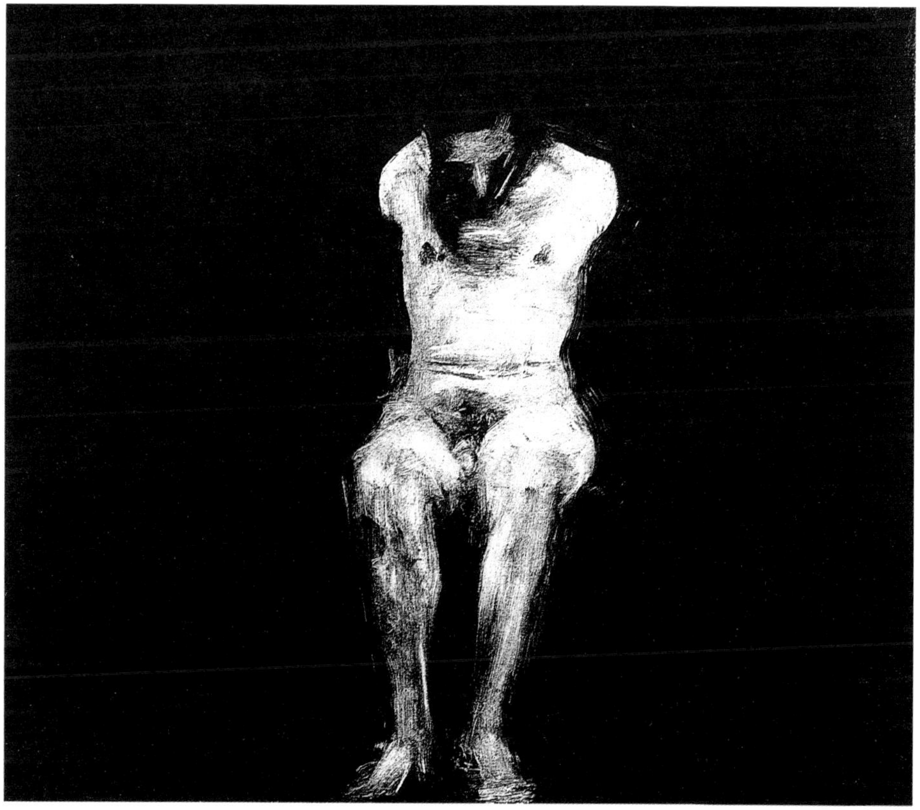

STEPHEN P. HAYES
Man 12, 1993
Monotype, 6¾" × 7¾"
Courtesy of Elizabeth Leach Gallery

PANEL STATEMENT

As evidenced by the submissions we considered, contemporary American painting continues to mirror issues of social and political change. However, it also reflects a strong, renewed interest in art that is beautiful and restorative. These artists reevaluate traditions of landscape, still life, and narrative painting; they explore the relationship between representation and abstraction; and they seek to infuse painting's vocabulary with philosophical, social, and subjective concerns. Yet the craft and care in work and materials are integral to their process, demonstrating that painting still embodies their passion for tactility and the distinctiveness of human touch.

Perhaps because these artists live in the West, landscape painting emerged frequently, often juxtaposing historical conventions and recent conceptual approaches to evoke the psychic importance of the land. Also, we were pleased to see submissions from mural painters whose genre is also associated with the West, and particularly the Southwest, where it reasserts the tradition of social content and direct involvement of artists with their communities.

THE PAINTING PANEL
Suzanne Delehanty,
Curator/Museum Consultant
Benito Huerta, Artist/Curator
Lynn Taber-Borcherdt, Artist
Michele Zackheim, Artist

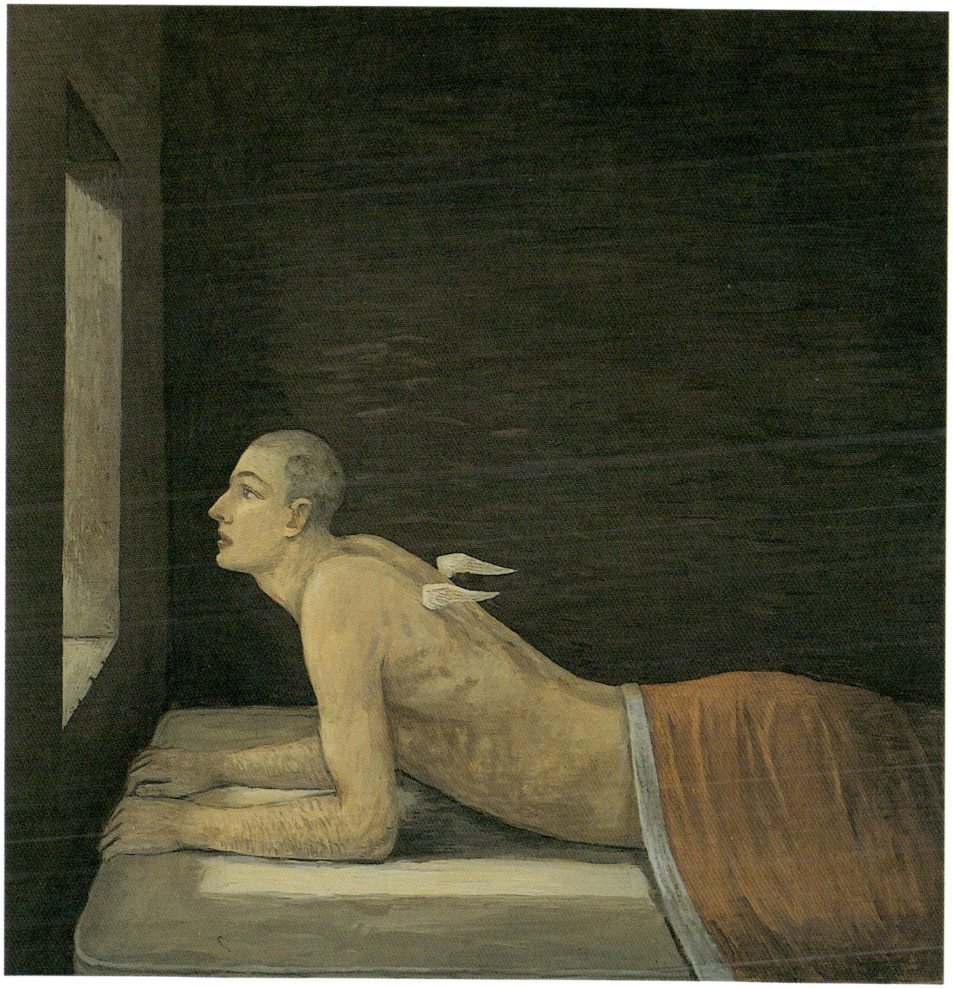

PAUL GREEN
Flaw, 1994
Acrylic on wood, 16" × 16"
Collection of Larry and Debbie Kline

DIANE ANDREWS HALL
The Thought of Sight, 1993
Oil on wood, 3 panels,
10″ × 10″ × 2″ each
(32 panels installed and
viewed as one piece)

CHRISTOPHER T. TERRY
Ventilator, 1993
Oil on canvas, 40″ × 34″
Courtesy of
Contemporary Realist Gallery

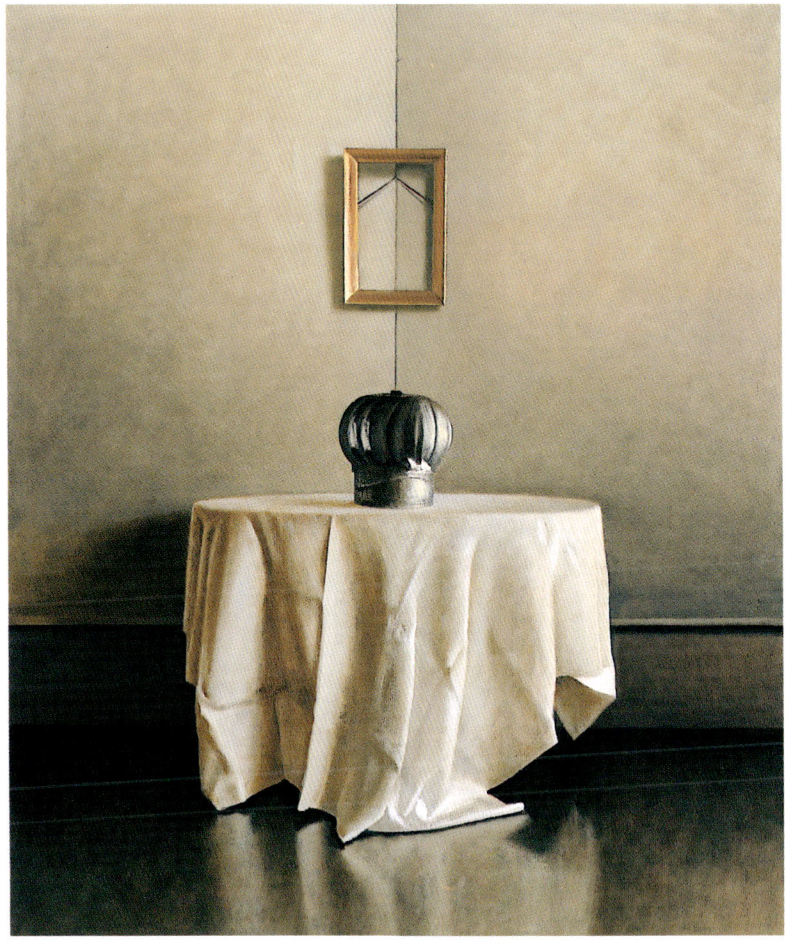

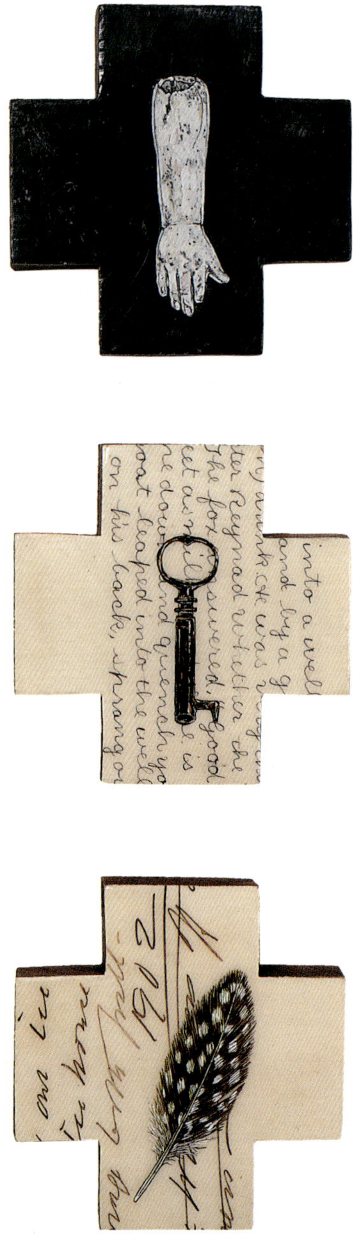

KENNA MOSER
Relic #6: arm fragment, key, and feather, 1993
Beeswax, vintage text, and oil paint on redwood
3 panels, 4″ × 4″ each
Courtesy of Susan Cummins Gallery

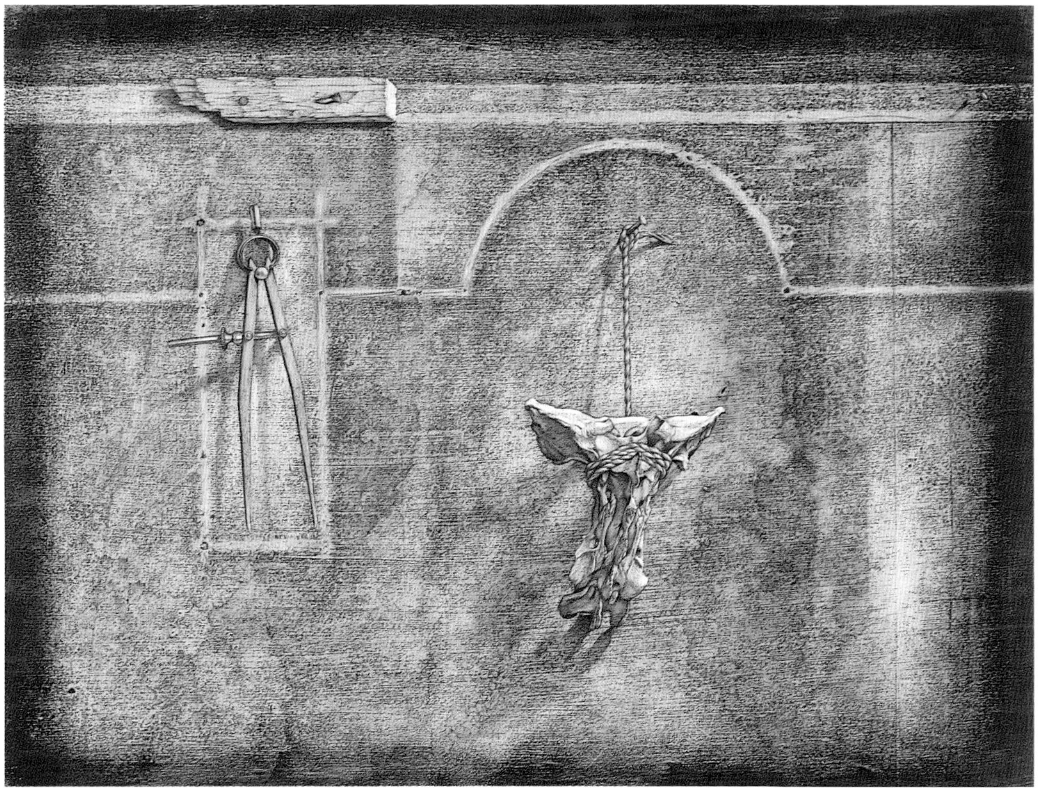

GREGORY SCHULTE
Sacred Sacrum, 1994
Graphite and gesso on paper,
21" × 28"

PANEL STATEMENT

Through experiments and investigations within the framework of new technological developments, these artists question the hierarchy of our cultural assumptions, grappling with the domains of scientific, industrial, and commercial endeavors even at points where these systems seem most impervious to dialogue. They resist dependence on one medium or material, circumventing commodification of their work and generating aesthetic and ideological alternatives to authoritative norms through their content, method, media, and criticality.

We found a courageous poeticism in much of this work. The artists reveal an enormous amount of self through their obsessions and failures, which sometimes are the impetus of the work itself. They thereby articulate the strained dialogue between humanist traditions and technology, exposing an expansive fallibility in the areas where intention exceeds accomplishment while pointing to the value of doubt, inquiry, and participation.

THE NEW GENRES PANEL
Steve Barry, Artist
Mary MacArthur Griffin, Curator/Consultant
Bruce Yonemoto, Artist

JAMES L. ACORD
Artist Working with Scientist on Art Project, 1992 (right)
Monstrance, work in progress (left)
Granite, 60″ × 28″ × 13″

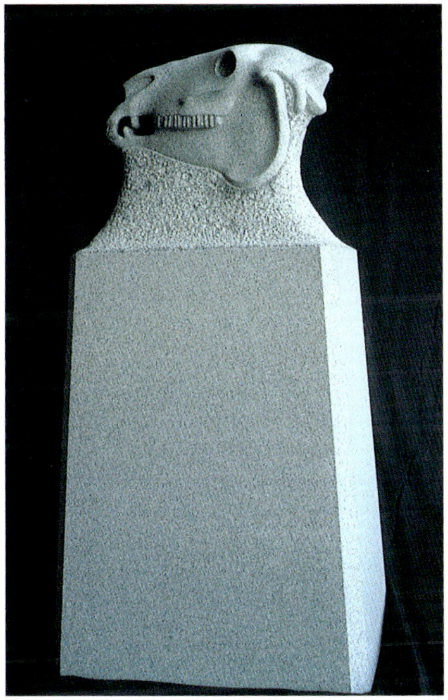

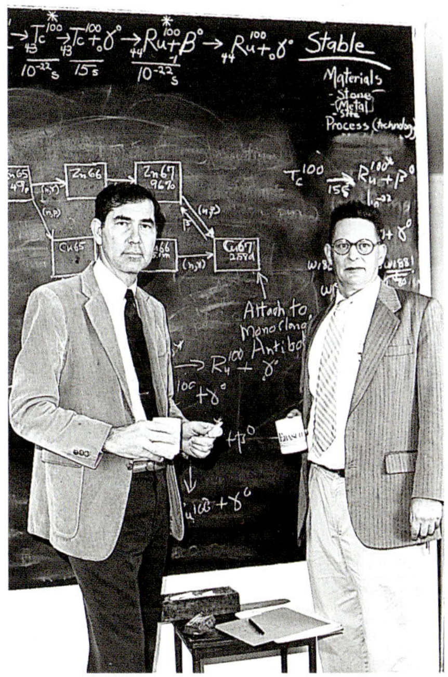

It's our Nuclear Age.
The Age of Stone lasted 50,000 years,
the Age of Bronze 8,000 years,
the Age of Iron 2,000 years, and we're
46 years into the Nuclear Age.
(Excerpt of text from performance/ presentation at the Seattle Art Museum, January 14, 1992)

I am on my coffee break. The acrid beverage jars my weary senses. One of the guys on the early shift scorched this coffee in a dirty pot two hours ago. Now they're all on the roof, in the biting chill of winter, rebuilding a cooling tower pump. I'm left to answer all the tenant calls. Ordinarily I'd feel left out. I love to rebuild large unwieldy pumps. But the misting spray of the cooling tower is toxic, filled with heavy metals and biocides. I've had my fill of that. Alone in the break room I can relax. My feet are throbbing and sore, swollen inside my steel-toed work boots. I roughly place them on the table. There's no one here to offend. They're all upstairs bonding beneath the spray of rancid condenser water. (Pump, *1993)*

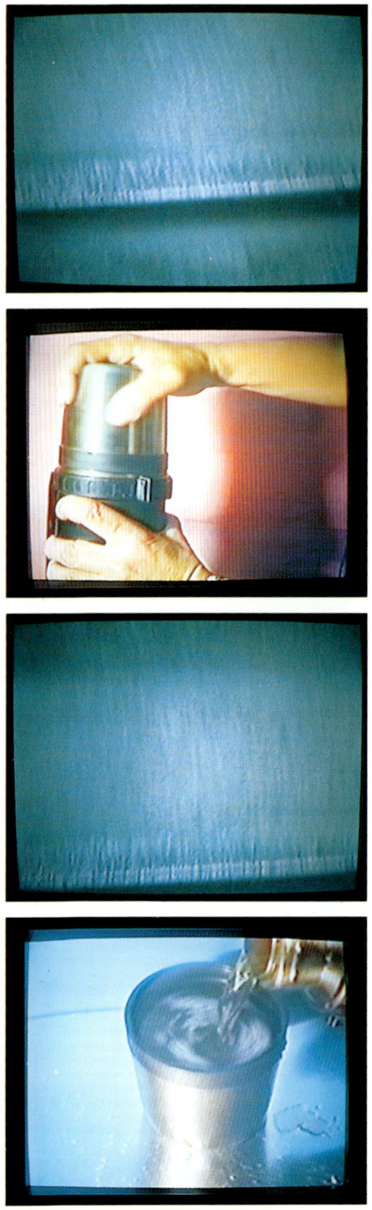

CINTHEA FISS
Pump, 1993
Installation, 10′ × 15′ × 17′

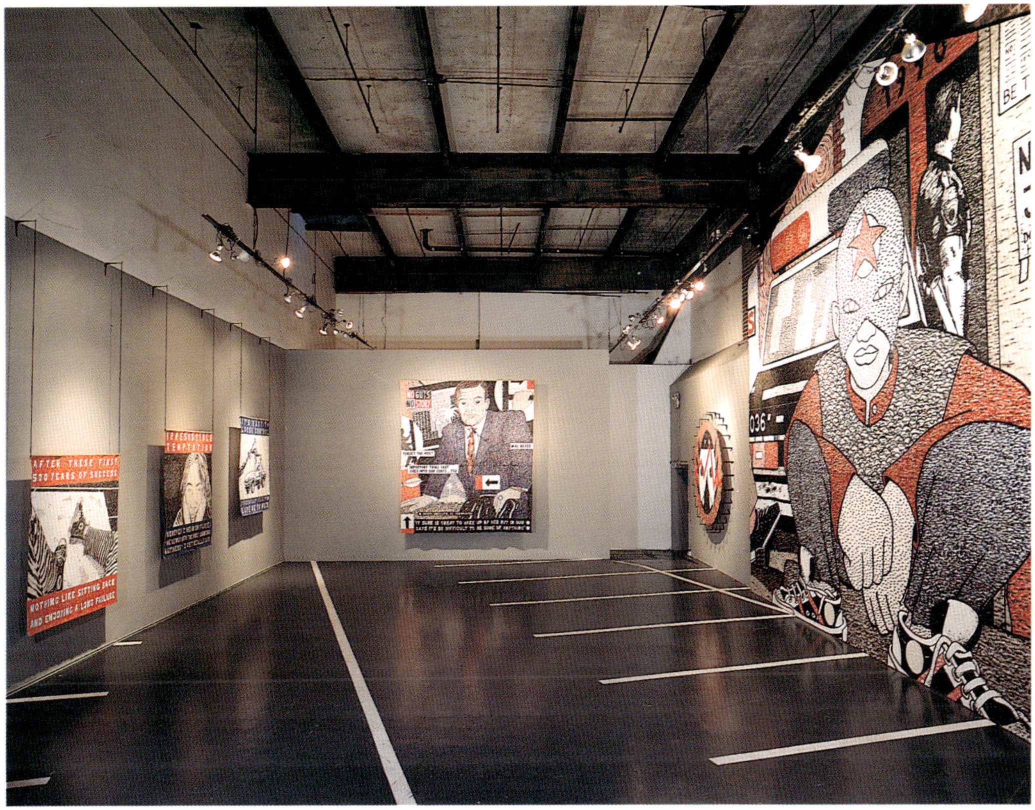

RIGO 94
Adprop-one dream come two, 1992
Installation with painted floor,
walls, and canvases, 30′ × 25′ × 60′

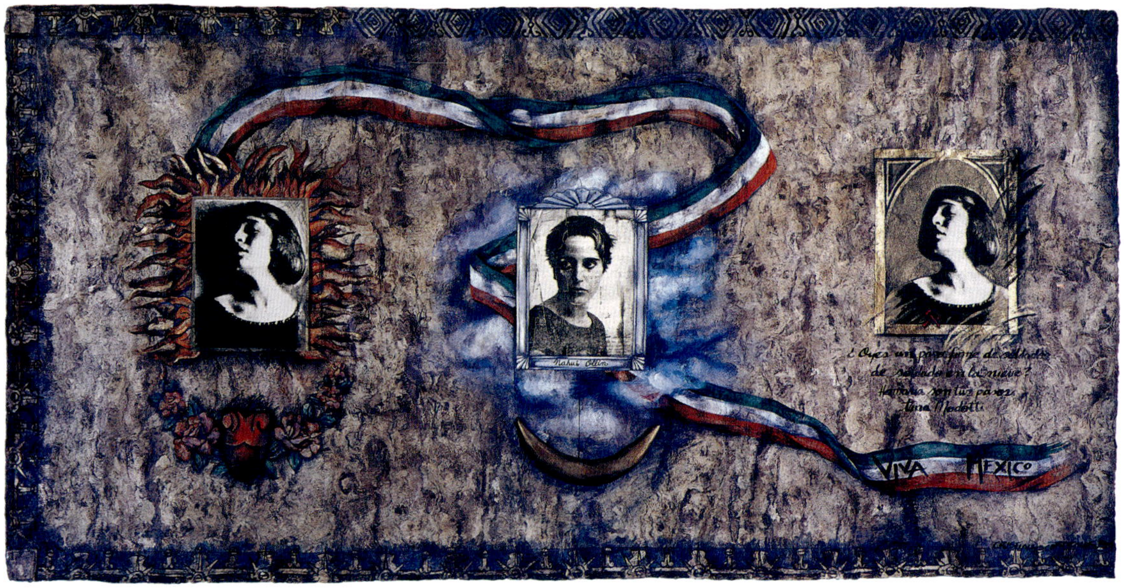

CRISTINA CARDENAS
Cuando Duele el Corazón, 1994
Gouache, acrylic, lithography,
wood on bark paper, 47" × 95"

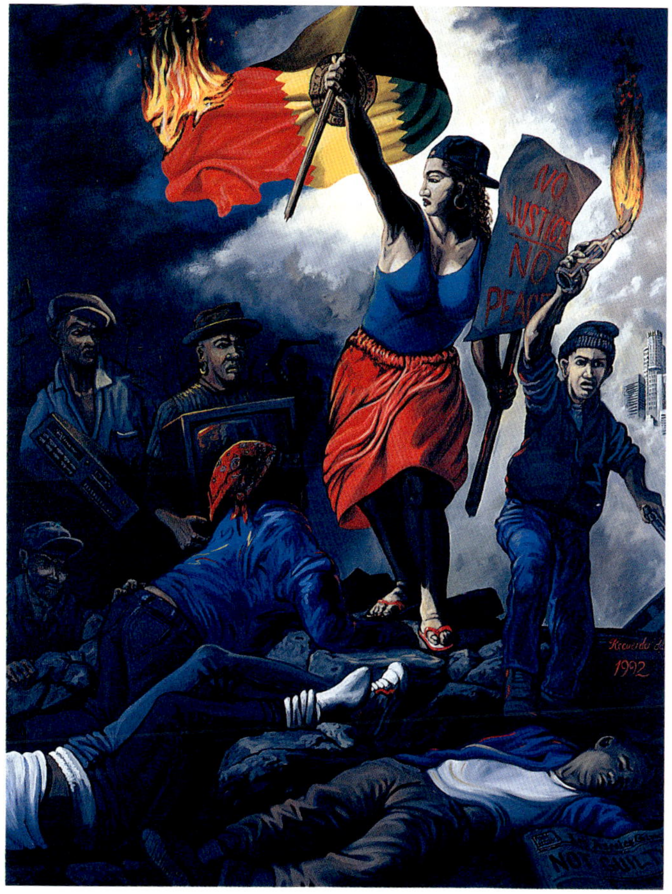

SANDOW BIRK
Injustice Leading Greed and Opportunity, 1992
Oil on canvas, 68″ × 53″
Collection of Mr. Brad Allan

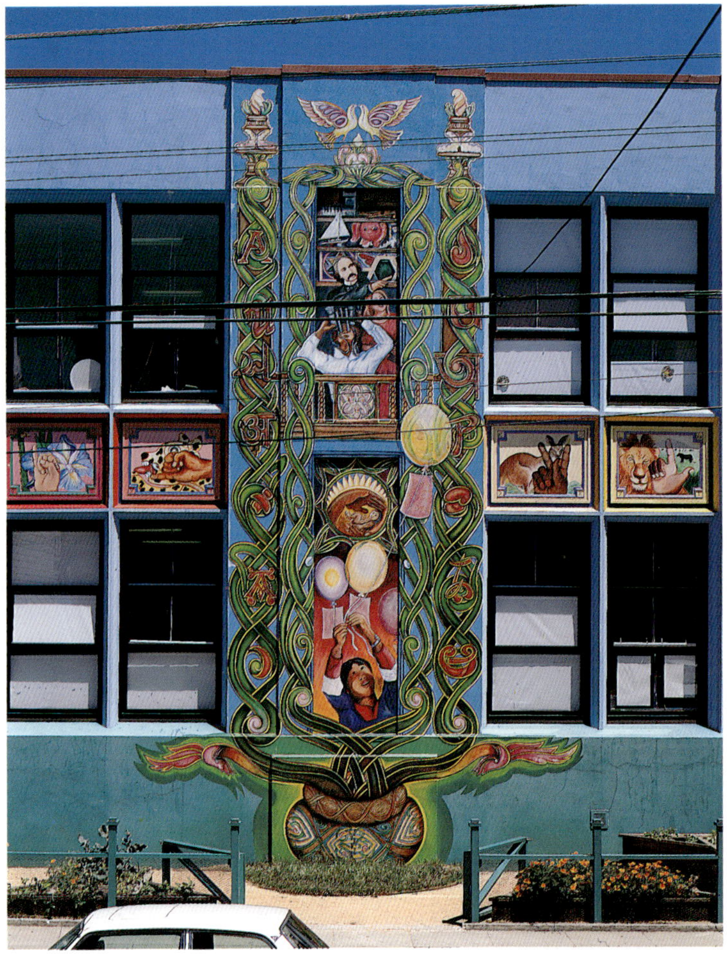

SUSAN KELK CERVANTES
The Silent Language of the Soul
(detail), 1990
Acrylic on stucco
32′ × 300′

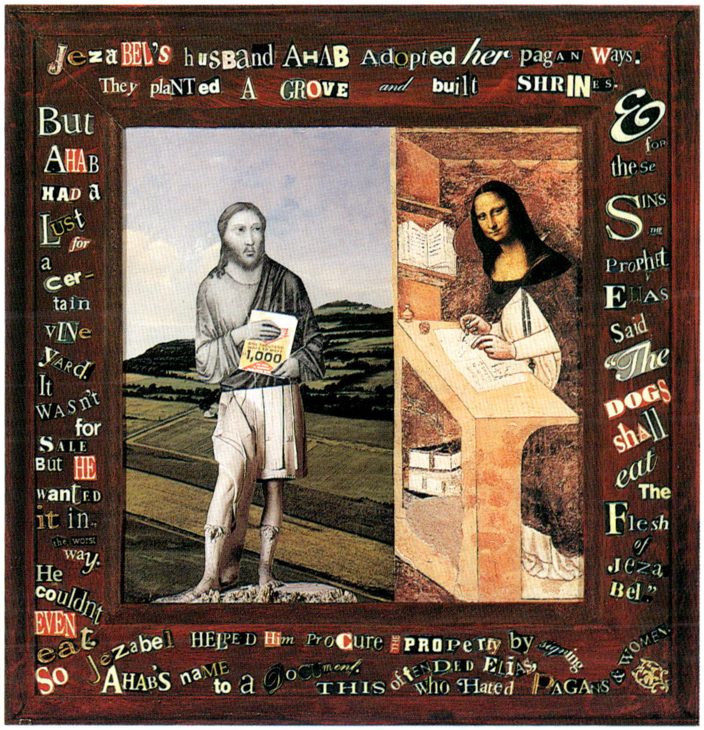

DEBORAH F. LAWRENCE
Jezabel Series #2, 1993
Paper collage, linoleum, wood,
13″ × 13″

PANEL STATEMENT

Numerous innovative, and essentially all traditional, ways of working on paper were exhibited by the portfolios we reviewed. Yet we found ourselves consistently drawn to work that demonstrated a strong personal vision. Although these artists acknowledged the traditions of art making, we selected those who we felt reached past the usual limits of technique and medium as an outgrowth of that vision.

In many works we noted a devotion to the exploration of ideas and images deep within the psyche through the physical process of creating and an effort to investigate questions of cultural and personal identity through the intimacy of working on paper. In general, we found the work chosen to be quite personal and original, prompted by inner spirit rather than outer experience.

THE WORKS ON PAPER PANEL
Allen Edmunds, Artist
Wayne Kimball, Artist
Charlotta Kotik, Curator,
The Brooklyn Museum
Aida Mancillas, Artist

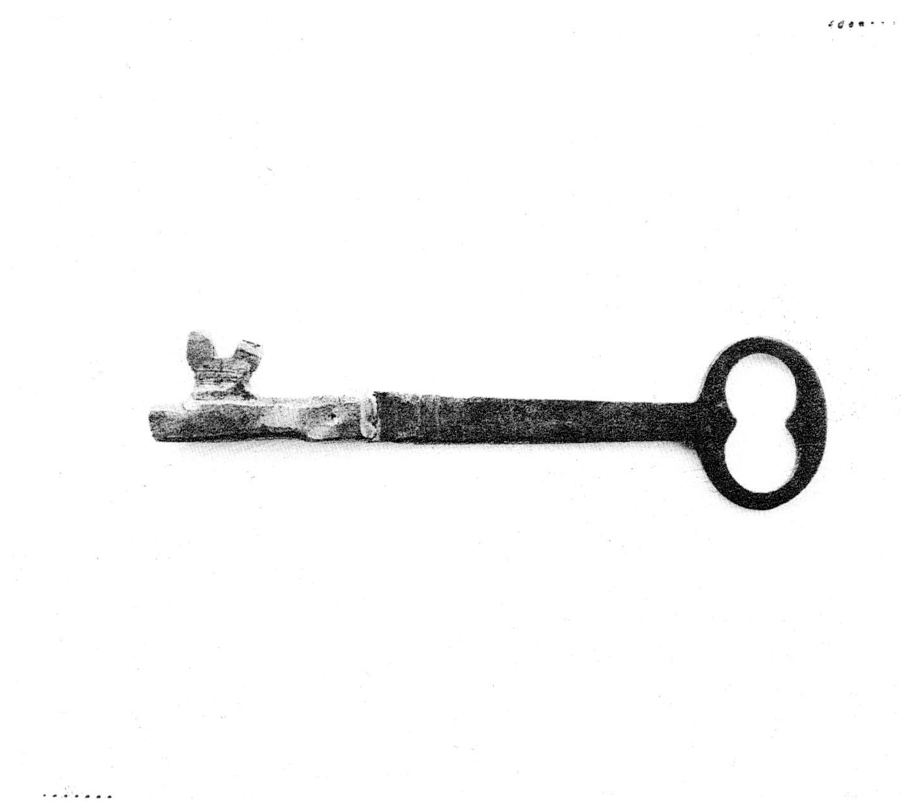

SUSAN MAGNUS
Untitled #19, 1993
Photogravure, unique impression
paper size: 16½" × 16½"
image size: 3¾" × 4¾"

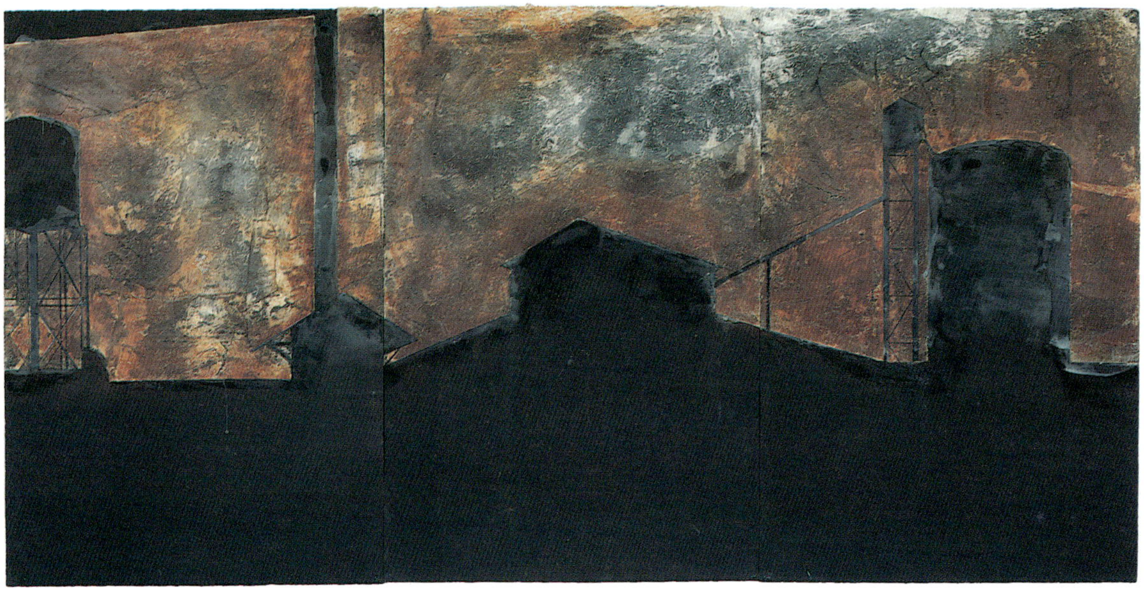

JOSÉ LUIS RODRÍGUEZ
Citadel, 1992
Charcoal on paper, 44″ × 90″

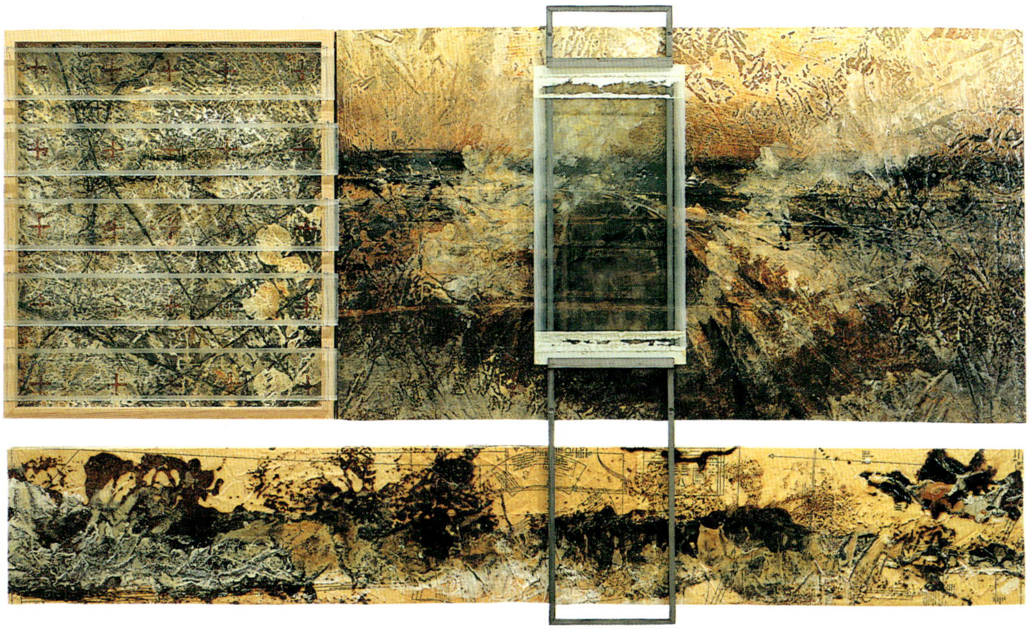

CANAN TOLON
Theodolite, 1993
Acrylic on canvas with wax, garment patterns, Turkish coffee grounds, glass, and steel, 44″ × 80″ × 3″

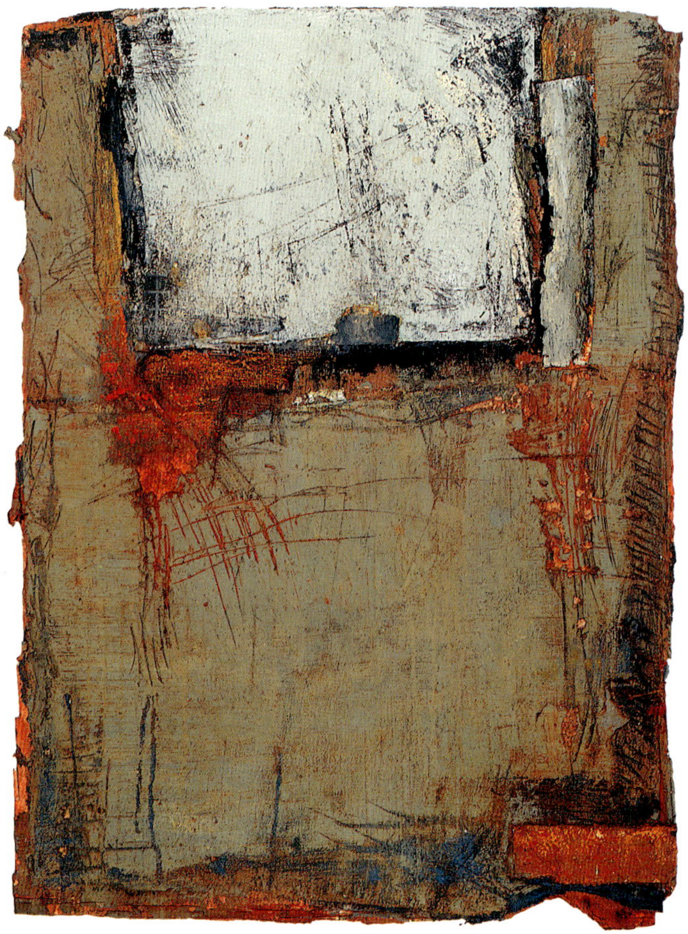

DAVID GREEN
Rear Window Site #5, 1992
Acrylic and pastel on paper, 30″ × 22″
Collection of RayChem Corporation

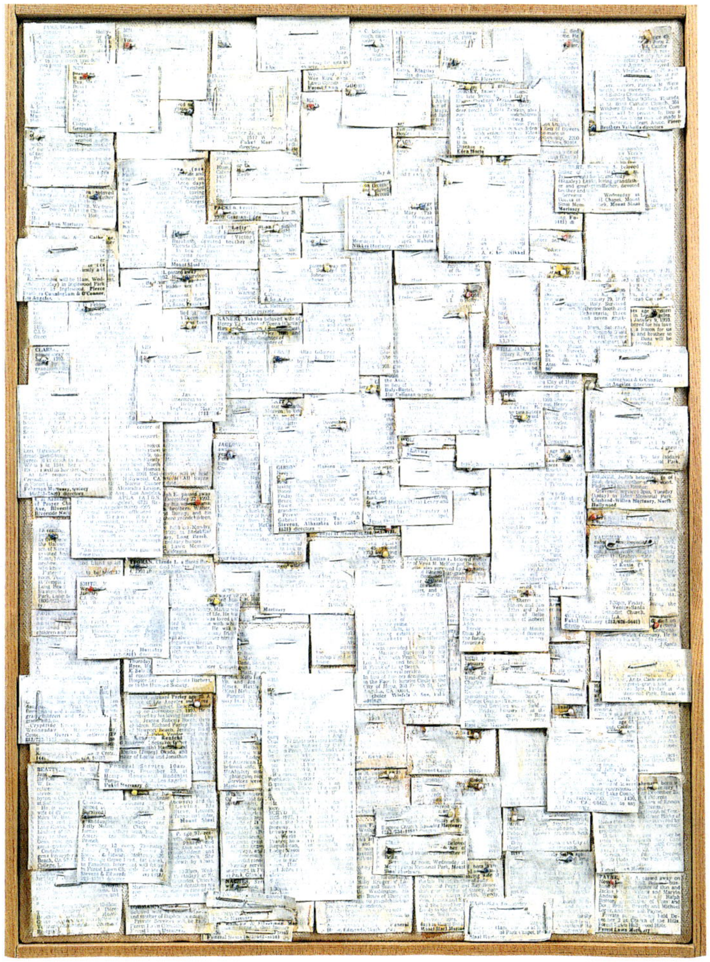

KEVIN MILLER
Untitled, 1993
Oil, obituaries on canvas, 17½″ × 12½″
Collection of Joni and Monte Gordon

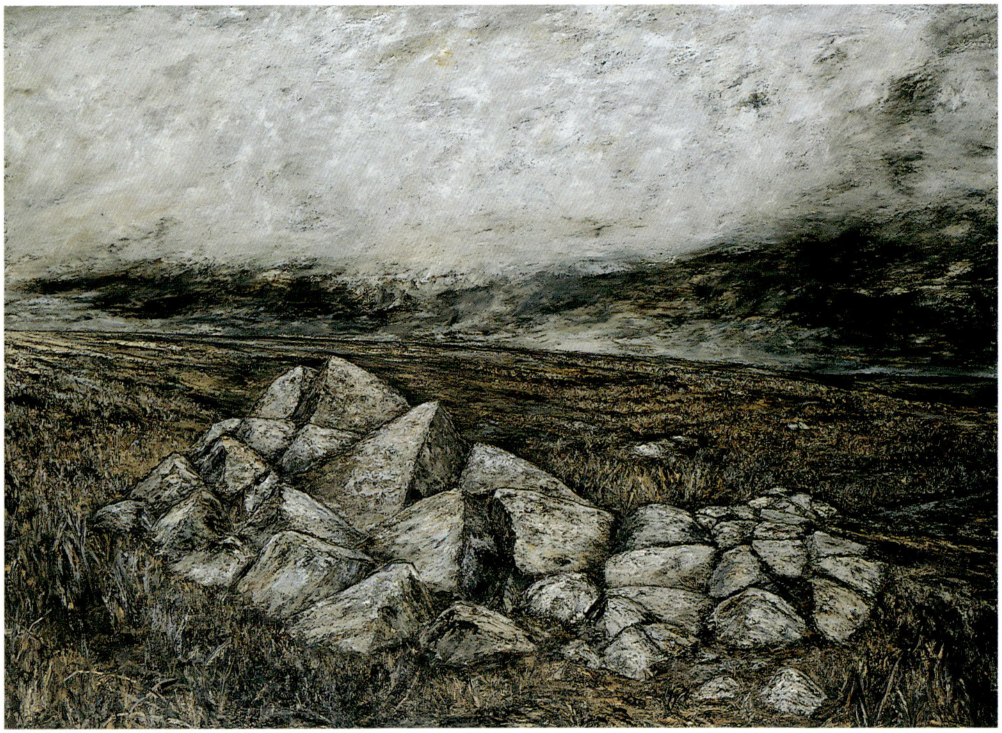

EV THOMAS
Headland Marker, 1993
Oil on canvas, 60″ × 84″
Collection of Julie and Conrad Prusak

MICHAEL MARLOWE
Sharing Fluids, 1992
Oil paint and tar on paper,
105″ × 55″ × 3″
Courtesy of
Elaine Horwitch Gallery

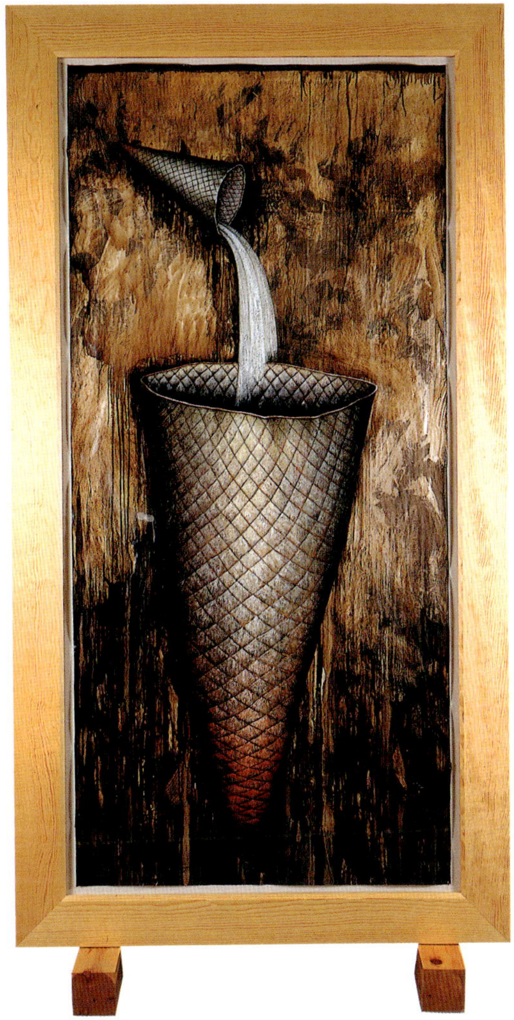

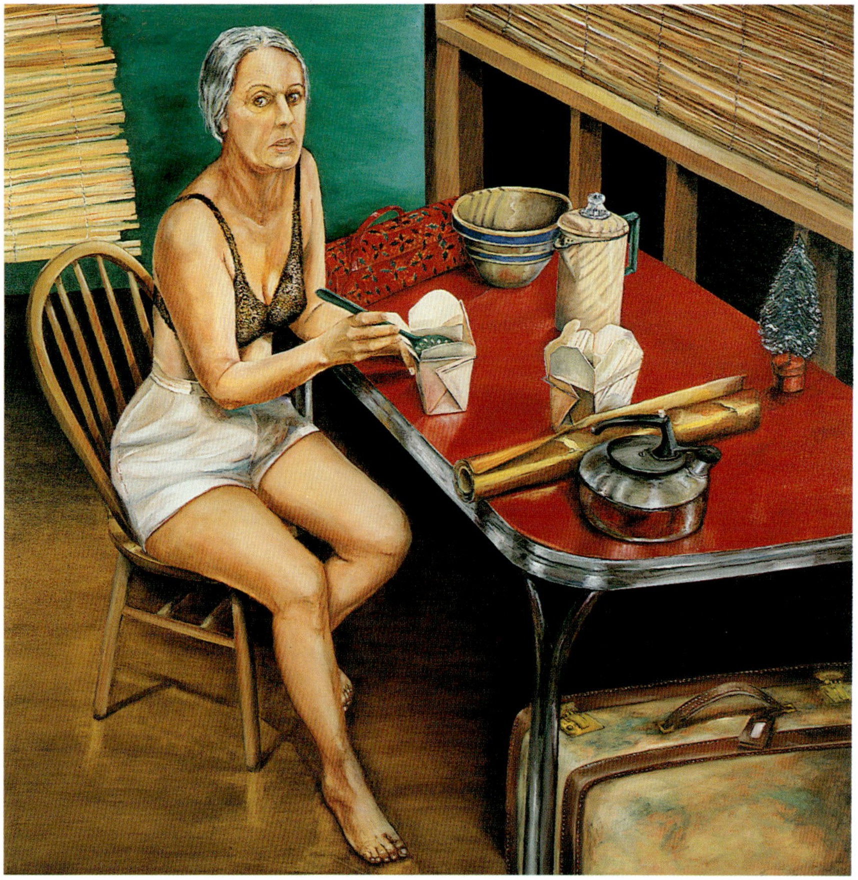

PAT WARING SHERWOOD
Christmas Dinner, 1994
Oil on canvas, 54″ × 54″

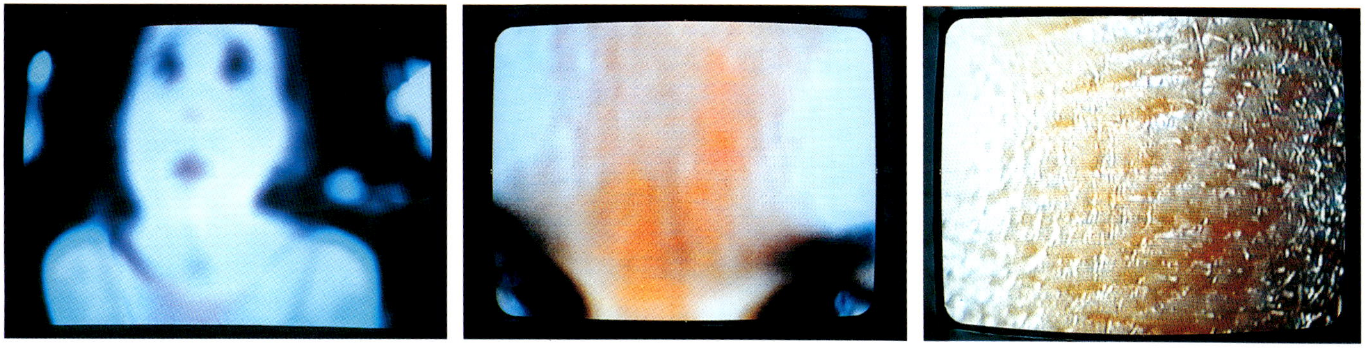

JEAN RASENBERGER
What I'm After, 1994
A sequence of images
using a lipstick camera
Videotape, color,
mono sound, 10 minutes

THE ARTISTS

With Artist Essays

by Kathleen Shields

JAMES L. ACORD

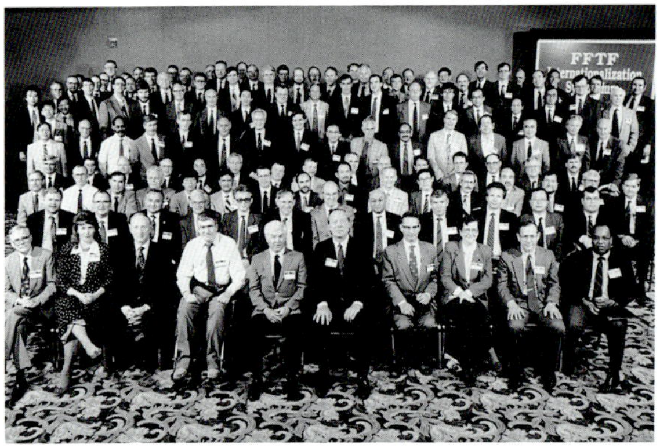

ARTIST WITH SCIENTISTS, *1992*
Performance
12′ x 30′ x 24′

Combining his training in metal and stone sculpture with a fascination for nuclear technology, James Acord makes installations and does "performance/presentations" that evolve from his objective "to interject the discipline of art into the decision-making process of societies' use of nuclear technology" and "to create sculpture uniting civilization's traditional aesthetic concerns with its advanced materials, processes, and technologies." Over the course of a five-year residency at the Hanford Nuclear Reservation in Washington State, Acord has been involved in an elaborate collaborative project with the scientists and engineers there, has been issued "the only Radioactive Materials License for the creation of art," and has become one of the smallest private owners of uranium.

In addition to his residency project, which "transmutes a radioactive fission product to a stable (non-radioactive) isotope and incorporates it into stone and advanced metal alloy sculpture," Acord creates installations which have the look of folk art but the content of a sophisticated nuclear vocabulary. He also gives his performance/presentations to science and art groups around the country, publicly articulating his vision and completing his form of ongoing performance art that incorporates his themes as effectively as any one medium. KS

Selected Individual Exhibitions

Documents: Five Years at Hanford, Two Bells, Seattle, Washington, 1994

Chronicals: Nuclear Materials into Art, Hoffman Gallery, Portland, Oregon, 1993

Transmutations/Art in a Nuclear Age, Spokane Art School Gallery, Spokane, Washington, 1991

Moving to Richland, 911 Arts Center, Seattle, Washington, 1989

Selected Group Exhibitions

Forest of Visions—Artists and the Environment, Knoxville Museum of Art, Knoxville, Tennessee, 1993–1995

Yes in My Backyard, Allied Arts Gallery, Richland, Washington, 1993

Non-Patented Artists-Made Machines, Corvallis Arts Center, Corvallis, Oregon, 1991

Low-Tech, Center on Contemporary Art, Seattle, Washington, 1990

Selected Awards

Art Matters, Inc., New York, New York, 1994

Regional Artist's Projects Grant, On the Boards, Seattle, Washington, 1993

Born 1944 in Seattle, Washington

Nuclear Engineering, Washington State University, Tri-Cities Branch, Richland, Washington, 1989, 1991

Stone Sculpture, Granite Cutters International Association, Barre, Vermont, 1979–1981

Sculpture, Cornish School of Art, Seattle, Washington, 1961

Resides in Richland, Washington

DENNIS L. ANGEL

First moved to paint by the experience of Edward Hopper's Gas Station, *Dennis Angel continues to be fascinated with "the depiction of a theatrical light/space and its psychological and emotional implications." His paintings (he also works in drawing and printmaking) have a strongly graphic quality and a strange, almost surreal or artificial-looking luminosity that contribute to their appearance as stage sets. The narratives that are played out in these ambiguous scenes are incomplete and at times verge on the sinister, like a David Lynch drama or a de Chirico setting. A consistent motif is a swimming pool in the desert with one or two figures engaged in some mysterious activity. The eerie light comes from the pool lights below the surface of the water, as well as from sunsets, lightning storms, firework displays, or even the aurora borealis in twilight or night skies. Angel's limited palette, focusing on blues and greens with touches of red or yellow or stripped down to black and white, heightens the mood of isolation and remoteness. And the typically distant, flat horizons combined with small, nondescript figures enhance the vast loneliness of the space, as well as an emotional solitude: "The spaces in my paintings are intended to be private, the viewer or audience participating from outside, remaining separate and as voyeur."* KS

Selected Individual Exhibitions

Vestiges, Governor's State University, Infinity Gallery, Chicago, Illinois, 1994

The Abandoned Arena, Blue Sky Gallery, Portland, Oregon, 1993

Dennis Angel, Recent Work, Lite Rail Gallery, Sacramento, California, 1992

Paintings and Drawings by Dennis Angel, Contemporary Art Workshop, Chicago, Illinois, 1988

Selected Group Exhibitions

Contemporary Issues of Self, Museum of Art, University of Oregon, Eugene, Oregon, 1994

55th Annual National Exhibition of Contemporary American Painting, The Society of the Four Arts, Palm Beach, Florida, 1994

Re: Make/Re: Model, Deson Saunders Gallery, Chicago, Illinois, 1993

Stockton National Print and Drawing Exhibition, The Haggin Museum, Stockton, California, 1992

Peculiar People Pictures, R. H. Love Contemporary, Chicago, Illinois, 1991

Current Works 90, Leedy-Voulkos Art Center, Kansas City, Missouri, 1990

Selected Awards

Artist in Residency Fellowship, LIED Discovery Museum, Las Vegas, Nevada, 1994

Juror's Award of Distinction, Rockville Art Museum, Rockville, Maryland, 1993

UPDC Research Grant, University of Wisconsin, Stevens Point, Wisconsin, 1991

Gallery Affiliation

Eva Cohon Gallery, Chicago, Illinois

Born 1955 in Chicago, Illinois

M.F.A., Indiana University, Bloomington, Indiana, 1988

B.F.A., University of Oklahoma, Norman, Oklahoma, 1985

Parson's School of Design, New York, New York, 1974–1976

Resides in Henderson, Nevada

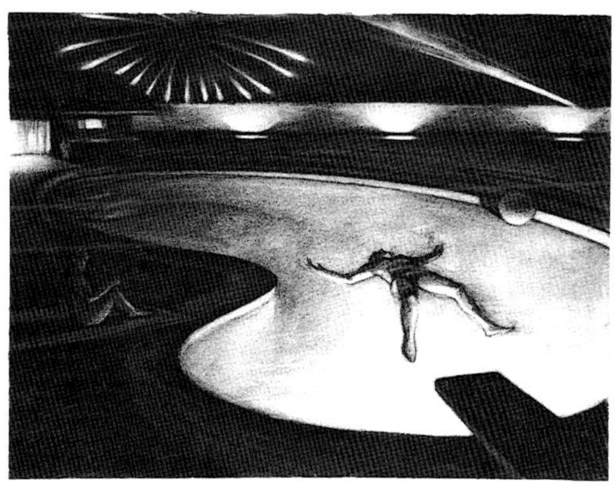

4TH OF JULY, *1993*
Charcoal on paper
12" x 16"

MAURA BENDETT

Maura Bendett's fragile compositions seem to evolve outward from a center, like many of the biological and natural forms that influence her work. Usually most dense in the middle, her vocabulary of delicately drawn cellular structures, plant forms, and other Miro-like squiggles seems to float in a space that is only partly limited by the borders of the canvas. Each rectangle could almost be a view through a microscope in which organisms drift and evolve. But Bendett is also interested in the physical properties of form and incorporates such materials as spices, shellac, and beeswax into her paintings. She says she started using saffron, for example, "because I liked the way it stained the canvas when used in combination with water, and because of its conceptual qualities as a real biological stamen of a flower."

Lyrical and intimate, Bendett's works convey her curiosity and delight in nature's processes. For her, the process of making paintings holds a similar wonder. As she "reinvents" painting for herself through the incorporation of different materials, various techniques, spontaneous markmaking, and the creation of multiple layers, she reenacts the sense of discovery she feels with nature. Through her works, which then become like recordings of her own process and state of mind, she hopes to invoke in the viewer a corresponding experience of the beauty and wonder of the creative process. KS

Selected Individual Exhibitions

domestic setting, Los Angeles, California, 1994

Dennis Anderson Gallery, Los Angeles, California, 1989

Selected Group Exhibitions

domestic setting at The Lobby Gallery, The Lobby Gallery, New York, New York, 1994

Current Abstractions, Barnsdall Art Park, Los Angeles Municipal Art Gallery, Los Angeles, California, 1994

One Nail, 1529 Wellesley, Los Angeles, California, 1993

Not Men, TRI, Los Angeles, California, 1992

Eye to Eye, Cirrus Gallery, Los Angeles, California, 1989

Vex, Helen Lindhurst Gallery, University of Southern California, Los Angeles, California, 1987

Vex II, North Gallery, Otis School of Art, Los Angeles, California, 1987

Selected Awards

Sydney A. Temple Award, The Art Council of the Wight Art Gallery, UCLA, Los Angeles, California, 1985

University Grant, The School of Fine Art, UCLA, Los Angeles, California, 1984

Born 1961 in Long Island, New York

M.F.A., UCLA, Los Angeles, California, 1987

B.A., UCLA, Los Angeles, California, 1984

Resides in Los Angeles, California

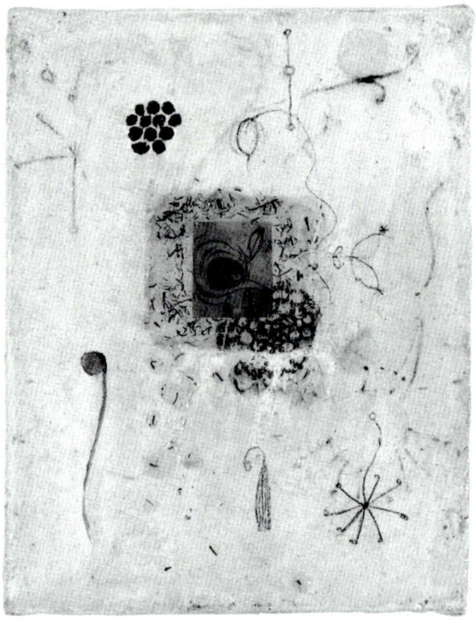

UNTITLED (Etching with Saffron and One Blueberry), *1994*
Oil, ballpoint pen, salt, saffron, etching, resin on canvas
10¼" x 8" x 1"

SANDOW BIRK

Working from the belief that "it is essential for art to have social and historical relevance beyond the art world," Sandow Birk paints contemporary urban situations in classical, art historical settings. In particular, he depicts actual events or circumstances in the inner city of Los Angeles where he lives, often focusing on the events that occurred there in 1992 and that manifested that city's "frequent, inevitable clashes and overlaps of various cultures and their effects on each other."

Combining his commitment to community and the contemporary with a strong background in 17th- and 18th-century European painting, Birk portrays such events as The Death of Manuel, *an apparent victim of a drive-by shooting, in the format of Ingres's* Death of Marat; *or the composition of* The Truce Between the Crips and the Bloods *as reminiscent of Rembrandt's* The Night Watch. *Although it is not necessary to be aware of Birk's specific art historical references, the complexity, drama, and grandeur of his pictures confer a sense of dignity and even heroism upon his localized, contemporary subjects and lend them a universality that we all may understand.* KS

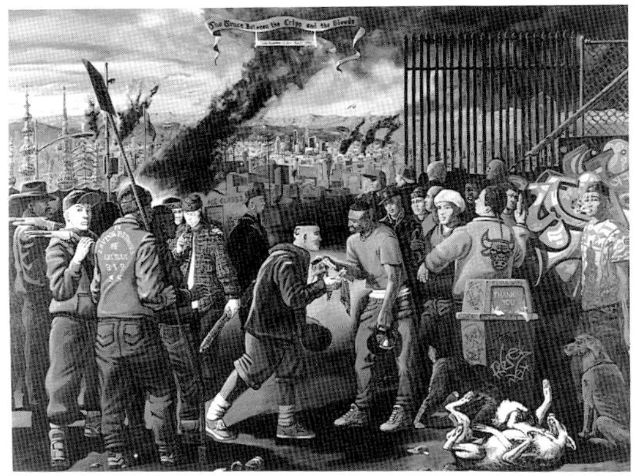

THE TRUCE BETWEEN THE CRIPS AND THE BLOODS—APRIL '92, *1993*
Oil on canvas
68" x 93"
Collection of Dr. William Levine

Selected Individual Exhibitions

Asphalt Landscape, Carl Hammer Gallery, Chicago, Illinois, 1994

Truce: Sandow Birk, Julie Rico Gallery, Santa Monica, California, 1993

The Gates of Hell: L.A. in the 90's, Orange Coast Gallery, Costa Mesa, California, 1992

Sandow Birk, Bess Cutler Gallery, Santa Monica, California, 1992

Selected Group Exhibitions

Crossing the Line, Delta Axis Contemporary Art Center, Memphis, Tennessee, 1994

Kustom Kulture, Laguna Art Museum, Laguna Beach, California, 1993

East Meets West, Speedway Gallery, Boston, Massachusetts, 1992

Contemporary Visions, Downey Museum of Art, Downey, California, 1991

Synthetic History, Parker Zanich Gallery, Los Angeles, California, 1991

Post Pop & Beyond, Bess Cutler Gallery, Santa Monica, California, 1990

Gallery Affiliations

Stuart Katz Contemporary Art, Laguna Beach, California

Carl Hammer Gallery, Chicago, Illinois

Morphos Gallery, San Francisco, California

Koplin Gallery, Santa Monica, California

Born 1964 in Pontiac, Michigan

B.F.A., Otis/Parson's Art Institute, Los Angeles, California, 1989

Painting, Bath Academy of Art, Bath, England, 1985

Painting, Parson's School of Design, Paris, France, 1984

Resides in Los Angeles, California

CRISTINA CARDENAS

Drawing on her background as a Latina artist born in Guadalajara, Mexico, and living in Tucson, Cristina Cardenas makes often large-scale paintings that reflect her desire to disrupt stereotypes of gender, religion, and race and to increase cross-cultural understanding. Working on canvas or bark paper which is made in Oaxaca, and incorporating acrylic, gouache, crayon, and lithography, she creates portraits of such mythical and historical figures as Coatlicue and Malinche, of actual people in her life, or of unnamed and unknown people. Gracefully rendering the human form and the drapery which frequently accompanies it, Cardenas's images have an almost classical character. Yet her figures may be presented in fragmentary situations, for example, El colgado *(The Hanging One), whose legs are all we see dangling above sharp metal spikes, or* Mujeres *(Women), who are shown from the waist down, seated, barefoot, and clothed in full skirts.*

The bark paper on which these works are painted gives them a mottled, decayed quality as though they were very old. Such works as Soldadera *(Soldier) and* Adelita*, with their icon-like images surrounding them, may even remind one of the Shroud of Turin and its sketchy, incomplete visage on ancient cloth. Thus combining multiple cultural references and styles and overlapping personal and traditional imagery, Cardenas's works are a tribute to identity as a multi-faceted, ever-changing condition.* KS

Selected Individual Exhibitions

Mujeres, Tucson Museum of Art, Tucson, Arizona, 1994

Cuando Duele el Corazon, Marspace Gallery, Phoenix, Arizona, 1994

Obra Grafica, Museo Regional de Oaxaca, Oaxaca, Mexico, 1991

Selected Group Exhibitions

La Frontera/The Border, Museum of Contemporary Art, San Diego, California, 1993–1994

Triennial, Contemporary Identities, Phoenix Art Museum, Phoenix, Arizona, 1993

Counter-Colonialismo, Centro Cultural de la Raza, San Diego, California, 1991–1993

Printmakers 1992, Social and Public Art Resource Center, Venice, California, 1992

Pasion por Frida, Casa Museo Diego Rivera, Mexico City, Mexico, 1992–present

Selected Awards

1992–1993 Great Walls Unlimited, Neighborhood Pride Mural Program, Social and Public Art Resource Center (SPARC), Venice, California, 1994

Artist Materials Grant, Phoenix Art Museum, Phoenix, Arizona, 1991

Fellowship in Painting, Tucson Pima Arts Council, Tucson, Arizona, 1990

Gallery Affiliations

Galeria Otra Vez, Los Angeles, California

Galeria Oaxaca, Oaxaca, Mexico

Born 1957 in Guadalajara, Mexico

M.F.A., University of Arizona, Tucson, Arizona, 1990

B.A., Universidad de Guadalajara, Guadalajara, Jalisco, Mexico, 1980

Architecture Studies, Instituto Tecnologico de Estudios Superiores de Occidente, Guadalajara, Jalisco, Mexico, 1980

Printmaking Studies, Instituto Allende, San Miguel Allende, Guanajuato, Mexico, 1979, 1981

Resides in Tucson, Arizona

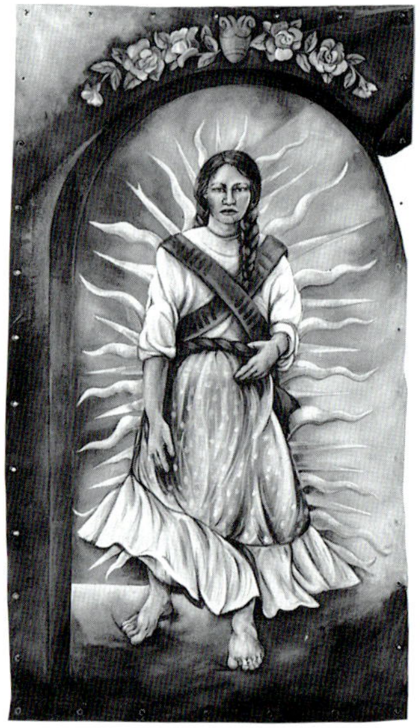

SOLDADERA (one of three images comprising triptich), *1993*
Acrylic, lithography on bark paper attached to canvas
95″ x 47″

SUSAN KELK CERVANTES

For more than twenty years Susan Kelk Cervantes has been painting public murals "with life-affirming themes offering a new view of art in our society." Her process, unlike that of the solitary artist in the studio, engages members of the community in which the mural is to be painted, not only allowing her to share her vision, skill, and knowledge, but encouraging those who will live with the mural in their daily lives to be a part of the creative process. The resulting imagery may therefore be a collaborative vision of the community's concerns, hopes, and dreams.

In Keep Our Ancient Roots Alive *the theme of the mural is native and immigrant contributions to the growth and vitality of the San Francisco Bay Area. It uses the giant sequoia tree—"the largest living thing on earth which only grows . . . in California"—as a symbol of "our many human lifetimes, and historical past and present." Cervantes conducted mural workshops with local elementary schoolchildren who then played an active part in designing and painting elements of the mural. Rich and colorful, it is steeped in the tradition of Mexican muralists and the more contemporary Southwest muralists who seek to make painting an integral part of people's lives; and it is a living document of the children's cultural ancestors, heroes, present lives, and hopes for the future.* KS

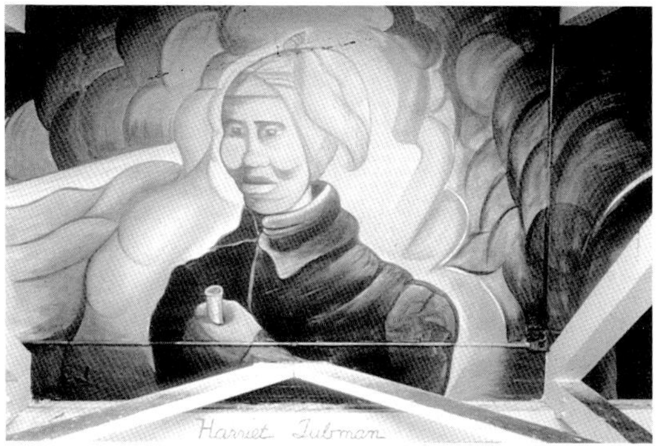

GREAT CLOUD OF WITNESSES
(detail), *1992*
Acrylic on plaster
6′ × 240′

Selected Individual Exhibitions (murals)

Maestrapeace, San Francisco Womens' Building, San Francisco, California, 1994

Fear and Hope, Clarion Alley, San Francisco, California, 1994

Keep Our Ancient Roots Alive, Cleveland School, San Francisco, California, 1994

Your Eyes Embrace My World, Rose Hotel, San Francisco, California, 1993

The Five Sacred Colors of Corn, Balmy Alley, San Francisco, California, 1991

The Silent Language of the Soul, Cesar Chavez School, San Francisco, California, 1990

Indigenous Eyes: War or Peace, Balmy Alley, San Francisco, California, 1990

Selected Group Exhibitions (murals)

Water Is Life, Vasilievsky Island, St. Petersburg, Russia, 1990

Food for the People, Community Food Resource Center, San Francisco, California, 1989

New World Tree, Mission Pool, San Francisco, California, 1987

Selected Awards

LEF Foundation Grant, Precita Eyes Mural Arts Center, San Francisco, California, 1993

Ronald McDonald's Children's Charities Grant, Precita Eyes Mural Arts Center, San Francisco, California, 1993

San Francisco Mayor's Office of Community Development Block Grant, Precita Eyes Mural Arts Center, San Francisco, California, 1993

Born 1944 in Dallas, Texas

M.F.A., San Francisco Art Institute, San Francisco, California, 1968

B.F.A., San Francisco Art Institute, San Francisco, California, 1965

Resides in San Francisco, California

TIMOTHY C. ELY

Working within the book form, Timothy Ely combines his multimedia drawings with a sculptural dimension to produce richly textured and colored objects. Using a wide range of materials including inks, watercolor, graphite, and metals in the drawings, and leather, metals, paints, resins, stone, bones, and pigment in the bindings, he provides a densely tactile experience for the viewer/participant that is made even more intimate through the small scale and sequential process of discovery that is part of enjoying any book.

Ely is closely involved with the histories of bookmaking and artists' materials, continually exploring such traditional printing methods as engraving and etching, as well as more contemporary, technical means of image-making. His works therefore embody for him both an objective and subjective investigative process: "My books are about the co-mapping of personal and historical experiences—which happens at a conscious and unconscious level—and how the merger of those experiences conspires to provide visual metaphors out of which a complicated life can be understood. My imagery reflects my interest in cartography, used as a way of viewing the landscape, from above, and as a way of locating ideas in psychological space. I also explore my interest in artifacts of human history—which allow us to invent stories about our past. The bookworks become personalized atlases of arcane pasts and futures." KS

Selected Individual Exhibitions

Black Maps & Synesthesia, Granary Books, New York, New York, 1993

Artist Books, Victoria & Albert Museum, London, England, 1989

Books & Drawings, Contemporary Crafts Gallery, Portland, Oregon, 1988

Selected Group Exhibitions

Books as Objects, Comus Gallery, Portland, Oregon, 1993

The Painted Book, Gallery Tinka, San Jose, Costa Rica, 1992

(Ely & Dürer) Early Views & Star Charts, Firestone Library, Princeton University, Princeton, New Jersey, 1992

Contemporary American Bookbinding, Bibliothèque de l'Arsenal, Paris, France, 1990

Book Arts in the U.S.A., Center for Book Arts, New York, New York, 1990

Delire de Livres, Cultural Center, Boulogne-Billancourt, France, 1989

Selected Awards

Fellowship, Art Matters, Inc., New York, New York, 1988

Fellowship, Pollock-Krasner Foundation, New York, New York, 1986

Visual Artists Fellowship, National Endowment for the Arts, Washington, District of Columbia, 1981

Gallery Affiliation

Granary Books, New York, New York

Born 1949 in Snohomish, Washington

M.F.A., Design, University of Washington, Seattle, Washington, 1975

B.A., Drawing, Printmaking, Western Washington University, Bellingham, Washington, 1972

Bookbinding, Private Tutorial, David Sellars, Daphne Beaumont, Wright, England, 1982

Resides in Portland, Oregon

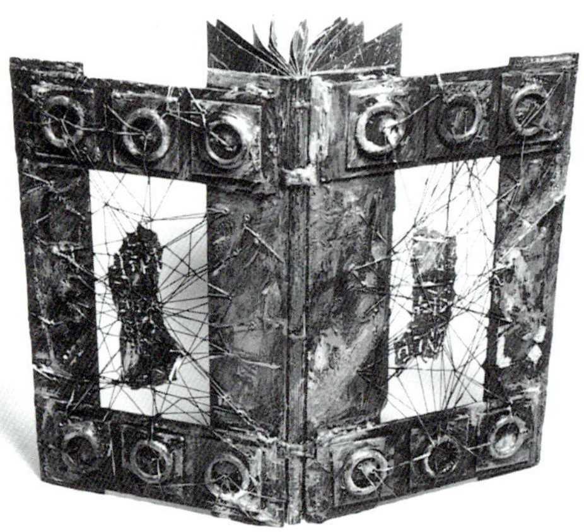

BORDERLINE 2, *1989*
Artist book—mixed media (paper, thread, resin, pigments, gold)
10" × 7½" × 1" (closed)
Private collection

DOROTHY A. FAISON

Dorothy Faison works with shallow, often discontinuous pictorial spaces in which she places images of primary symbols and objects. Tents, caves, house shapes, boats, and coffins carry a universal reference to passages in life and death while the part-landscape, part-maplike treatment of space merges the visual with the symbolic. In Separate Isle, *for example, a group of personal and cultural images occupies the right side of the composition, as though along the shore of the large expanse of water to the left, but in the flattened out perspective, they also read as a map's legend. In* Leaving Antigone, *sketchy lines and peripheral images of tents or dwellings give the painting a diagrammatic quality while the loosely painted surfaces provide a handwrought character for her imagery. She has used an actual tent ceiling as a support, as in* Ancient Dwelling (Tent) Fragment, *and may incorporate wax, charcoal, watercolor, and even dog hair into her works.*

Sometimes reminiscent of pre-Renaissance depictions of space or perhaps Native American ledger drawings, Faison's compositions also reflect a postmodernist return to so-called "primitive" impulses. Through such references she works to "combine the power, mystery, and purpose of primitive tribal art and medieval icons within the context of contemporary painting and life." KS

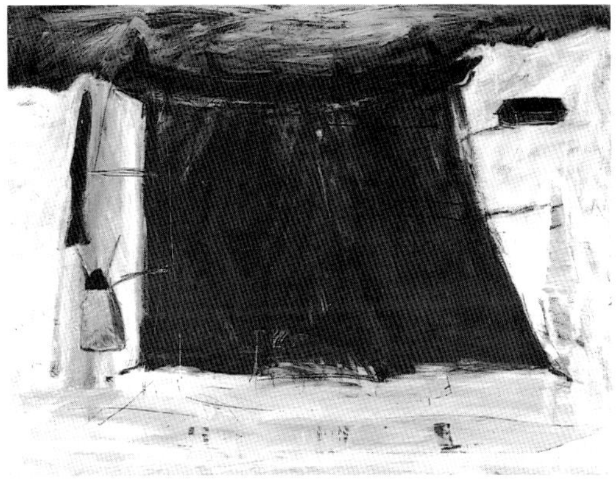

ONE WORD, *1993*
Oil, charcoal, wax on masonite
36" × 48"

Selected Individual Exhibitions

First Biennial, The Contemporary Museum, Honolulu, Hawaii, 1993

Cox Prize Exhibition, Recent Work, Honolulu Academy of Arts, Honolulu, Hawaii, 1990

Some of Us Are Just Born Different This Time with Shoes, Kapiolani CC Koa Gallery, Honolulu, Hawaii, 1988

Selected Group Exhibitions

Artists of Hawaii, Honolulu Academy of Arts, Honolulu, Hawaii, 1986–1993

Quincentennial Invitational, Honolulu Academy of Arts, Honolulu, Hawaii, 1992

Advertiser Gallery 30 Years, The Contemporary Museum, Honolulu, Hawaii, 1991

Selections 1990, Honolulu Advertiser Collection, The Contemporary Museum, Honolulu, Hawaii, 1990

Crossings '89, Fondation Mona Bismark, Paris, France, 1989

Kunsan International Drawing Show, Kunsan University, Kunsan, Korea, 1986

LIS '81, Lisbon International Drawing Competition, Museum of Modern Art, Lisbon, Portugal, 1981

Selected Awards

Melusine Award for Painting, Honolulu Academy of Arts, Honolulu, Hawaii, 1993

Catherine Cox Award for Excellence in the Visual Arts, Honolulu Academy of Arts, Honolulu, Hawaii, 1989

Born 1955 in Schenectady, New York

M.F.A., Intermedia, Otis Art Institute, Los Angeles, California, 1979

B.F.A., Drawing and Painting, University of Hawaii, Honolulu, Hawaii, 1977

Fine Art, Edinburgh College of Art, Scotland, United Kingdom, 1975–1976

Art History, University of Edinburgh, Scotland, United Kingdom, 1974–1976

Art History, Sophia University, Tokyo, Japan, 1973

Resides in Kailua, Hawaii

CINTHEA FISS

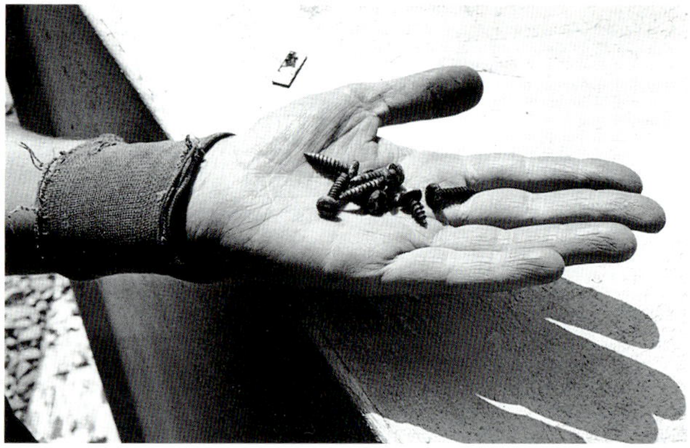

SCREWS FROM PUMP, *1993*
Type c print
16" x 20"

For the past four years Cinthea Fiss has examined her ten years of experience as a stationary engineer—a boiler plant and heating/ventilation/air-conditioning mechanic in a high-rise office building—through video, photography, text, and installation. As an artist and blue-collar worker, she is interested in "constructing a space in the male-dominated trades. I am compelled to depict the structure of the pernicious relationships of power in which I work."

In Pump *Fiss uses an installation including video, audio, and photographs to present different perspectives of "the socially constructed picturing of women." Through photographs of women's hands at work; a video depicting a repetitive, close-cropped view of stairs being climbed, accompanied by two soundtracks inventorying tools, machinery, and other aspects of the workplace; and an environment made dim and overly warm with small aluminum lamps and an electric heater, Fiss works to create an "eroticized" space in which "the desire for control over that erotic imaging is stressed." In* Tradesecrets *a spoken text combined with projected images articulates the dangers faced by those who practice her trade. Many of the photographic images are of hand tools—Fiss' and those of Jessica, another female stationary engineer—while the text narrates a disturbing, first-person account of the hazards (some work-related, some gender-specific) of Fiss' job.* KS

Selected Individual Exhibitions

Pump, Side Street Projects, Santa Monica, California, 1994

Sabre 620 Series, Eye Gallery, San Francisco, California, 1984

Selected Group Exhibitions

Breakdown, Cyberspace at EZTV, Los Angeles, California, 1993

Honeycakes for the Cerebus, Beyond Baroque, Venice, California, 1993

American Film Institute National Video Festival, Los Angeles, California, 1993

Breaking Barriers: Revisualizing the Urban Landscape, Santa Monica Museum of Art, Santa Monica, California, 1992

Some Federal Reserve Notes, Foundation for Art Resources, Los Angeles, California, 1992

Six American Photographers, Sunny Gate Gallery, Taipei, Taiwan, 1991

Selected Awards

Bay Area Video Coalition Artist Equipment Access Award, San Francisco, California, 1994

American Association of University Women Fellowship Award, Los Angeles, California, 1990

San Francisco Art Commission Purchase Award, San Francisco, California, 1985

Born 1955 in New York, New York

M.F.A., California Institute of the Arts, Valencia, California, 1993

B.F.A., Antioch University, Yellow Springs, Ohio, 1978

American Photography Institute National Graduate Seminar, Tisch School of the Arts, New York University, New York, New York, 1993

Local 39 Stationary Engineers Apprenticeship, San Francisco, California, 1982–1986

Nova Scotia College of Art and Design, Halifax, Nova Scotia, 1979–1980

Resides in Berkeley, California

KAY FRENCH

Kay French's paintings of vast skies above flat land and water horizons are metaphors for states of mind and the timeless dichotomies that are symbolized by the relationship of earth and sky. Including only a thin strip of land or water to ground her image, she nearly fills the canvas with lushly painted, atmospheric compositions of clouds, dust, smoke, wind, storms, and clearings reminiscent of Turner or Ryder. She draws her imagery from art history but also from the newspaper, weather books, her own surroundings, and memories: "My desire is to create an image that strikes a chord of recognition rooted solidly in the present without forsaking the past."

The relatively small format of her paintings seems to contain the roiling puffs and stippled patches of atmosphere within their edges. This balance between substantiality and dematerialization holds many layers of reference to relationships that interest French: those between the pragmatic and the romantic, rationality and the imagination, the physical and the spiritual. They also blur the area between representation and abstraction. Read as both images of the landscape and expressive objects of sensation and emotion, French's paintings invoke a wide range of responses through a simple but focused subject. KS

Selected Individual Exhibitions

Pulliam/Deffenbaugh/Nugent, Portland, Oregon, 1994

Drypoints, Artisan Gallery, Akron, Ohio, 1987

Land, Water, Sky, Artisan Gallery, Akron, Ohio, 1986

Selected Group Exhibitions

Crosscut—Oregon Biennial, Portland Art Museum, Portland, Oregon, 1993

Urgent Nostalgia, Center of Contemporary Art, Seattle, Washington, 1993

ART SEATTLE, Westin Hotel, Seattle, Washington, 1993

ART LA, Los Angeles Convention Center, Los Angeles, California, 1991

Gallery Affiliation

Pulliam/Deffenbaugh/Nugent, Portland, Oregon

Born 1953 in Lansing, Michigan

B.F.A., Painting, Pacific Northwest College of Art, Portland, Oregon, 1986

B.A., Art History, Kent State University, Kent, Ohio, 1976

Resides in Portland, Oregon

BORDER, *1993*
Acrylic on wood
15" x 25"

DAVID GREEN

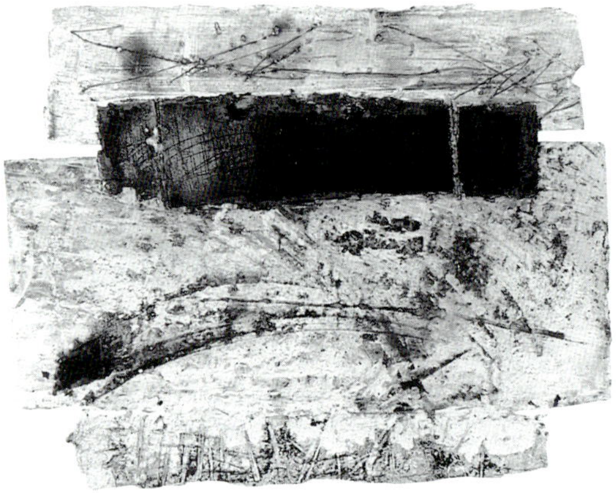

BLACK HINGE FRAGMENT #3, *1993*
Acrylic and oil pastel on paper
24″ x 30″ Collection of
Hewlett-Packard Corporation

Since childhood David Green has been fascinated with the textures, markings, and structures of old walls. He began by photographing abandoned farms, industrial buildings, and urban alleyways and eventually became interested in "a more metaphorical investigation of the influence of time on surfaces. Instead of reconstructing the surfaces of the walls and dealing strictly with aged objects as markers of time, I began to uncover the underlying symbolism inherent for me in my attraction to abandoned buildings, deteriorating walls, and discarded objects. A tangible sense of age, change, and the marks of time on human edifices all offer symbolic clues to the transitory nature of our individual existence."

The works are on roughly textured, eroded pieces of paper which look like richly hued, broken fragments of plastered walls. Green builds up layers of acrylic and sometimes collaged cheesecloth or cardboard, then scratches and abrades the surface in order to reveal underlying colors and textures and to create an appearance much like cracked and peeling old paint. Further distressing the surface with gestural marks which contribute movement to the compositions or, as in Black Hinge Fragment #3, *adding patch-like sections that seem to hinge discrete areas together, Green creates tactile objects that for him are "momentary embodiments of slowly changing surfaces, referring to our own bodies as we grow, change, weather, decline, and renew."* *KS*

Selected Individual Exhibitions

Archaeology of Moments, Lucy Berman Gallery, Palo Alto, California, 1993

Re: Guarding Site, Lisa Harris Gallery, Seattle, Washington, 1993

Fragments of Time, Lucy Berman Gallery, Palo Alto, California, 1991

Selected Group Exhibitions

Bird, Green & Sastre, Hewlett-Packard Corporation, Palo Alto, California, 1993

Pacific Northwest Annual, Bellevue Arts Museum, Bellevue, Washington, 1992

12th International Biennial, Whatcom Museum, Bellingham, Washington, 1992

Northwest Annual, Center on Contemporary Art, Seattle, Washington, 1990

Group Show, Western Washington University, Bellingham, Washington, 1990

Organic Truths/Civil Lies, 911 Contemporary Art, Seattle, Washington, 1989

Selected Awards

Installation Grant, 911 Contemporary Art, Seattle, Washington, 1989

Merit Grant, Ford Foundation, University of Washington, Seattle, Washington, 1978

Merit Grant, Ford Foundation, University of Washington, Seattle, Washington, 1977

Gallery Affiliations

Lisa Harris Gallery, Seattle, Washington

Lucy Berman Gallery, Palo Alto, California

Fresh Paint, Santa Monica, California

Born 1951 in Grants Pass, Oregon

M.F.A., University of Washington, Seattle, Washington, 1978

B.F.A., Ohio Wesleyan University, Delaware, Ohio, 1973

Apprenticeship, Bill Barrett, New York, New York, 1972

Resides in Seattle, Washington

PAUL GREEN

Paul Green's mysterious portraits evolve from an "image idea" that "precedes. . . knowledge of its meaning." Through them he hopes "to inspire empathy and to stimulate entry into a parallel world, a world that is not merely fanciful but that is endowed with the weight of metaphoric resonance." They are surrealist and literary in nature (Green often finds inspiration in reading), carrying a private symbolism for a sense of melancholy and solitude, but also faith and hope, through imagined conditions of the body. Let, *for example, echoes the serene pathos of Mantegna's 15th-century* St. Sebastian, *and* Lament *may recall a number of historical images of Christ in descent from the cross or as the object of mourning (e.g., Giotto's* The Lamentation*).*

Almost all of Green's figures are solitary and statuesque, their skin pale and translucent; we may perhaps interpret them as self-portraits. Their backgrounds are shallow and simple, even austere, and the palette muted but luminous, all contributing to a mythic timelessness that is nonetheless grounded in the personal and introspective. For the interpretation of these works is open to individual speculation. Their meanings remain obscure and almost otherworldly, and despite their literary sources they invoke a pre-verbal response that has as much to do with the body as with the mind. KS

Selected Individual Exhibitions

Lyons Wier Gallery, Chicago, Illinois, 1994

Laura Russo Gallery, Portland, Oregon, 1993

January Gallery, Fort Worth, Texas, 1993

Quartersaw Gallery, Portland, Oregon, 1991

Kiehle Gallery, St. Cloud, Minnesota, 1990

Selected Group Exhibitions

Gramercy Fine Art, New York, New York, 1993

Linda Hodges Gallery, Seattle, Washington, 1993

Wade Wilson Gallery, Chicago, Illinois, 1991

The Emotional Landscape, State of Illinois Gallery, Chicago, Illinois, 1991

Personal Symbols, Marylhurst Art Gym, Marylhurst, Oregon, 1989

Gallery Affiliations

Lyons Wier Gallery, Chicago, Illinois

Laura Russo Gallery, Portland, Oregon

Born 1960 in San Diego, California

M.F.A., Painting, School of the Art Institute of Chicago, Chicago, Illinois, 1989

B.F.A., Painting, Pacific Northwest College of Art, Portland, Oregon, 1985

Resides in Portland, Oregon

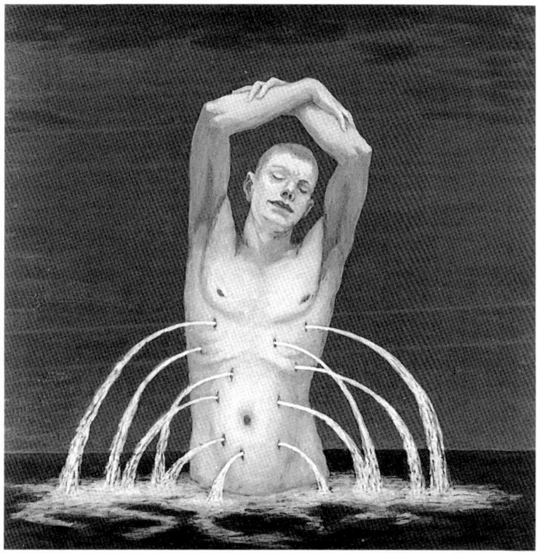

LET, *1993*
Acrylic on wood
16″ × 16″
Collection of Michihiro Kosuge

DIANE ANDREWS HALL

Diane Andrews Hall is interested in paintings as an experience of time, light, and movement and as a means of exploring perception itself. Her small oil paintings on wood are derived from cloud formations, dynamic weather patterns, and other atmospheric phenomena and are intended to be installed and viewed as one piece, as with The Thought of Sight, *a series of thirty-two paintings hung in a single horizontal line. Moving from one painting to the next, "the viewer becomes engaged in a self-conscious act of perception. . . . One might look up or down, through a camera or through dark glasses, be in a melancholic state or lost in memory, be wet from the mist or afraid in the dark. The act of seeing encompasses all the senses and becomes a psychology of seeing."*

The element of time and movement involved as one views each painting in succession lends a "cinematic quality" to Hall's work, which is offset by the sculptural quality of each two-inch-thick panel and the depth of surface produced by multiple layers of glazing. Thus each "block of atmosphere" is not only like a still from a film—an image or fragment from the process of seeing—but an object whose presence engages our own. For Hall, this allows herself and the viewer to be "a participant, not an observer. This gives me free rein to investigate the idea of 'a person' and to continue my interest in abstraction and representation, the dynamic and the static, and the fleeting nature of light." KS

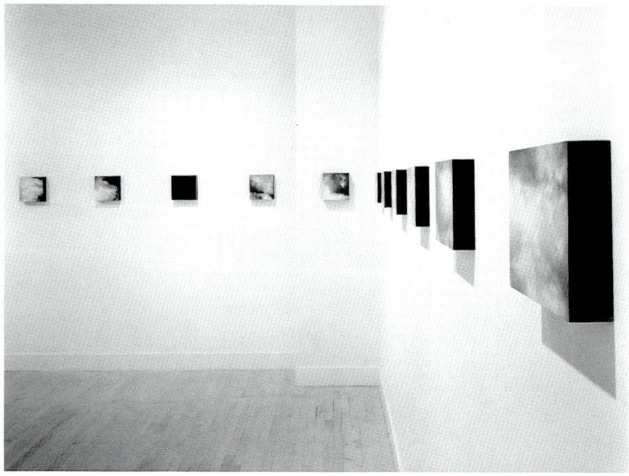

THE THOUGHT OF SIGHT, *1993*
Oil on wood—installation view
8" x 8" x 2"
32 panels installed and viewed as one piece
Courtesy of Haines Gallery

Selected Individual Exhibitions

The Thought of Sight, Haines Gallery, San Francisco, California, 1993

Diane Andrews Hall, Mincher/Wilcox Gallery, San Francisco, California, 1991

Not Knowing/The Absolute: Horizons, New Langton Arts, San Francisco, California, 1988

Diane Andrews Hall, Fuller/Goldeen Gallery, San Francisco, California, 1987

Diane Andrews Hall, Works Gallery, San Jose, California, 1984

Topography, Fuller Gross Gallery, San Francisco, California, 1989

Mystical Landscape, Maloney/Butler Gallery, Santa Monica, California, 1989

Selected Group Exhibitions

Facing Eden: 100 Years of Landscape Art in the Bay Area, M. H. de Young Memorial Museum, San Francisco, California, 1995

Why Painting, Susan Cummins Gallery, Mill Valley, California, 1992

Environmental Response, Falkirk Cultural Center, San Rafael, California, 1990

Selected Awards

Skowhegan School of Painting and Sculpture Fellowship Grant, Skowhegan, Maine, 1967

Gallery Affiliation

Haines Gallery, San Francisco, California

Born 1945 in Dallas, Texas

M.F.A., Hoffberger School of Painting/The Maryland Institute of Art, Baltimore, Maryland, 1969

B.F.A., Sophie Newcomb, New Orleans, Louisiana, 1967

Music, San Francisco Institute of Music, San Francisco, California, 1972–1975

Resides in San Francisco, California

STEPHEN P. HAYES

Stephen Hayes' mysterious and emotionally complex monotypes belie the simple process by which they are made. Using a reductive method of coating a plate with black ink and wiping it away with a rag, he forms nude figures in groups or alone, in various activities and postures, that for him "depict a range of feelings and actions from intimacy to alienation. I want them to portray the human condition as a complex one: sad, intriguing, humorous, hopeful, active, despairing, sensual, disgusting, lethargic, lost, confident, loving, boring, ever-changing, and vivid."

Although they have a curiously photographic look to them, perhaps due to their high-contrast, black-and-white palette, Hayes' images are not derived from photographs, models, or any other reference except his own thoughts and feelings. And while he chooses to work in black and white because "it makes the images appear more factual," he also wants "to create a place of mystery and indeterminate depth, populated by men and women in poses suggestive of actions not quickly understood." Man 12, *for example, a seated figure with arms hidden or truncated, seems emotionally and physically bound in despondent isolation. Or, in* Days of Love 3, *a couple is captured in what could be a lovers' embrace or a violent struggle. The background, as in all the images, is a dense black which only adds to the ambiguity of the scene, allowing us to imagine or choose the context for ourselves.* KS

Selected Individual Exhibitions

Paintings—Stephen Hayes, Papajon's Gallery/Restaurant, Kyoto, Japan, 1994

New Works—Monotypes, Elizabeth Leach Gallery, Portland, Oregon, 1994

Stephen Hayes—Monotypes, The Art Gym, Marylhurst College, Marylhurst, Oregon, 1993

Paintings—Stephen Hayes, Maryhill Museum, Goldendale, Washington, 1986

Selected Group Exhibitions

Crosscut, Portland Art Museum, Portland, Oregon, 1993

Oregon Biennial, Portland Art Museum, Portland, Oregon, 1991

Northern Lights, American Culture Center, Sapporo, Japan, 1991

Bumbershoot Festival, City of Seattle, Seattle, Washington, 1990

Panoramic Landscape, G. W. Einstein Gallery, New York, New York, 1987

James McLaughlin Memorial Exhibition, The Phillips Collection, Washington, District of Columbia, 1985

Gallery Affiliation

Elizabeth Leach Gallery, Portland, Oregon

Born 1955 in Washington, District of Columbia

M.F.A., Painting, University of Wisconsin, Madison, Wisconsin, 1980

B.S., Art, University of Wisconsin, Madison, Wisconsin, 1977

Resides in Portland, Oregon

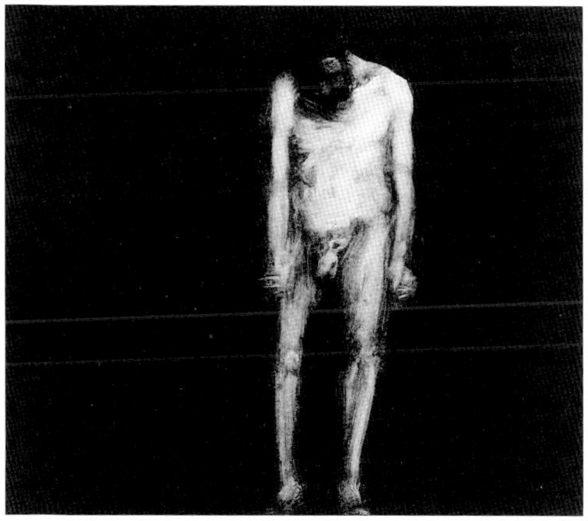

MAN 25, *1993*
Monotype
6¾" × 7¾"
Courtesy of Elizabeth Leach Gallery

DEBORAH F. LAWRENCE

Combining painting, collage, and text in her works on paper, Deborah Lawrence seeks to juxtapose historical and contemporary images and subjects in a way that informs both our past and present: "My job is to enhance the meaning of popular visual images by using them to tell stories and report on historical and current events. As I mature and evolve as an artist, the narrative changes, but it has always been a sort of running dialogue between me and my world. My frustration with the status quo, rebellion against political conservatism, impatience with the art establishment, disappointment in interpersonal relationships have all found their way into the compositions that appear on the surface to be telling a simple folk tale or twisting a cliche."

Lawrence's "Jezabel Series" underlies biblical and art historical motifs with such current issues as homosexuality, women in the priesthood, and other feminist concerns. While the images depict Jezabel as Leonardo's Mona Lisa *or at a table like that of* The Last Supper, *printed text collaged around each wide frame tells of episodes in Jezabel's life: her conflict with "men who worshiped Yahweh" and were disgusted by her "ancient, pagan" beliefs; her efforts to help her husband Ahab procure property he wanted, which offended the prophet Elias, "who hated pagans and women"; and ultimately her death by order of Jehu, of which nothing remained "but the skull and the feet and the extremities of her hands."* KS

Selected Individual Exhibitions

Solo Exhibition, Koslow Gallery, Los Angeles, California, 1990

Solo Exhibition, Koslow Gallery, Los Angeles, California, 1988

Solo Exhibition, Koslow Gallery, Los Angeles, California, 1987

Solo Exhibition, Riverside Art Center, Riverside, California, 1979

Selected Group Exhibitions

Miniatures, Olga Dollar Gallery, San Francisco, California, 1993

The Sticking Place: Space & Image in Contemporary Collage, Long Beach City College, Long Beach, California, 1992

Accretions: Collage & Assemblage, Space Gallery, Los Angeles, California, 1990

Terra Fluxus, California State University, Dominguez Hills, Carson, California, 1990

Dialogue Prague/Los Angeles, Lidovy Dum, Prague, Czechoslovakia, 1989

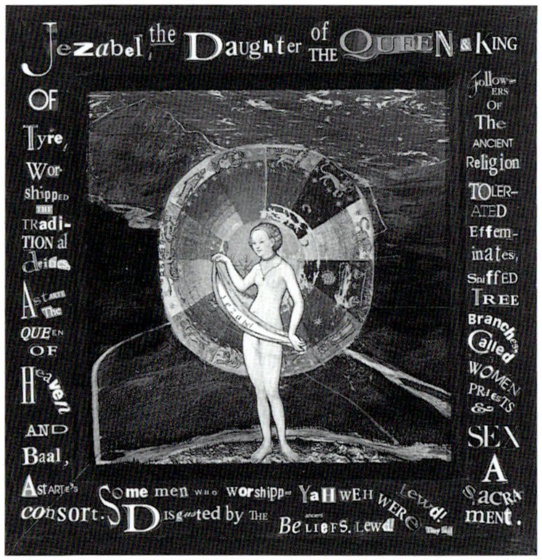

Selected Awards

Curator's Award, Northwest Annual, Seattle, Washington, 1994

Seattle Artists Visual Arts Program, Seattle Arts Commission, Seattle, Washington, 1993–1994

Individual Artist Grant, Los Angeles Department of Cultural Affairs, Los Angeles, California, 1990–1992

Gallery Affiliation

Olga Dollar Gallery, San Francisco, California

Born 1952 in Alhambra, California

M.F.A., Claremont Graduate School, Claremont, California, 1982

B.A., University of California, Riverside, California, 1976

Resides in Seattle, Washington

JEZABEL SERIES #1, *1993*
Paper collage, linoleum, wood
13" x 13"

SUSAN MAGNUS

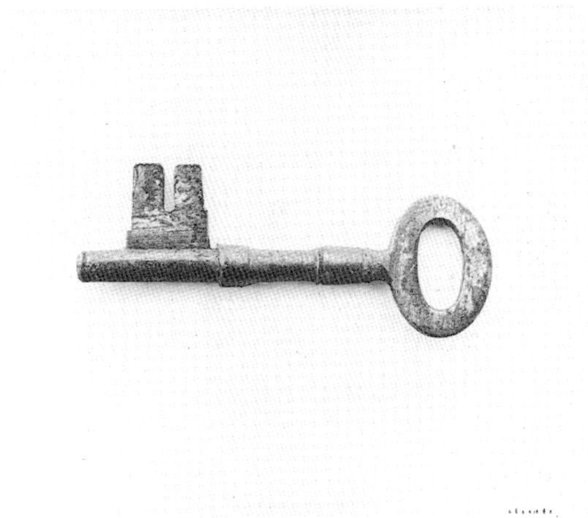

Untitled #2, 1993
Photogravure, unique impression
paper size: 16½" × 16½"
image size: 3¾" × 4¾"

Susan Magnus' series of thirty-three unique photogravure prints are intended to be installed in a large grid from the floor to the ceiling of one wall. Viewed in this configuration the similarities and subtle differences among the images of latchkeys may be seen, emphasizing not only the formal characteristics of each image but alluding to larger notions of reproduction and uniqueness. Using print-making, a method of producing multiples, to create a unique image enables Magnus metaphorically to explore issues of commodification and ownership: "The images of latchkeys, in this particular series, function as typologies or models and point to a society based on notions of possession—one in which a multitude of things physical and/or psychic may be locked away or hidden within."

While the latchkeys provide Magnus with a symbol from which many references may be extrapolated, they also offer a simple beauty in their sculptural form that speaks of age, use, and tactility. The photogravure technique not only gives them a photographic realism, capturing their three-dimensionality and surface details, but the printed surface of the paper lends an actual tactility to the works that—ironically—attracts us to them as objects. KS

Selected Individual Exhibitions

Rena Bransten Gallery, San Francisco, California, 1994

Rena Bransten Gallery, San Francisco, California, 1993

Selected Group Exhibitions

Wunderkammer, Rena Bransten Gallery, San Francisco, California, 1994

Object, Intersection for the Arts, San Francisco, California, 1993

Pro Arts Annual, Pro Arts, Oakland, California, 1993

Summer Exhibition, Rena Bransten Gallery, San Francisco, California 1993

Summer Exhibition, Rena Bransten Gallery, San Francisco, California, 1992

MFA Exhibition, Mills College, Oakland, California, 1992

Bay Area Student Photography, SF Camerawork, San Francisco, California, 1991

Buying the Magazine for the Ads, Terrain, San Francisco, California, 1991

Selected Awards

Jack and Gertrude Murphy Fellowship, The San Francisco Foundation, San Francisco, California, 1991

Alumnae Scholarship, Mills College, Oakland, California, 1991

Gallery Affiliation

Rena Bransten Gallery, San Francisco, California

Born 1957 in New York, New York

M.F.A., Mills College, Oakland, California, 1992

B.F.A., Parsons School of Design and the New School for Social Research, New York, New York, 1980

Resides in Emeryville, California

MICHAEL MARLOWE

Michael Marlowe's work reflects his twofold interest in objects: objects as represented in painted images and paintings as objects themselves. His use of a conical form is a means of "focusing on the issues of isolation, the dualities of nature, and the interaction of humankind. . ." Sometimes hollow, sometimes solid, painted as though constructed in a woven pattern, and placed in relations with other images, for example, a crown, seashells, or a skull, the cone provides a metaphorical vessel for human relationships and situations. The large size of the cone forms and their prominent centrality encourage an almost figurative reading, as though each is the protagonist in a little narrative that occurs on the richly painted surface. Each cone has an individual character as portrayed by its color, texture, and relationship to its background and the other images that accompany it.

Marlowe's presentation of these oils on paper conveys his concern for the literal objecthood of his works. They are often framed in wide, pine frames that sit on blocks and lean against the wall. This participation in the space of the room, combined with their human-sized scale and proportions (typically 105 inches by 55 inches), emphasizes their physical presence in relation to the viewer's own and brings Marlowe's interest in issues of the self in relation to the world into a more concrete realm. *KS*

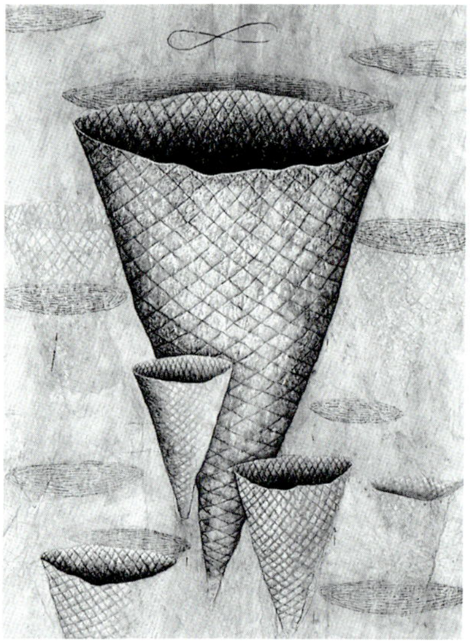

FLOATING VESSELS, *1993*
Oil paint, charcoal, concrete on paper
56" x 42"
Courtesy of Elaine Horwitch Gallery

Selected Individual Exhibitions

Recent Works, Scottsdale Center for the Arts, Scottsdale, Arizona, 1994

Elaine Horwitch Galleries, Scottsdale, Arizona, 1993

Malton Gallery, Cincinnati, Ohio, 1990

Selected Group Exhibitions

Shelter, Elaine Horwitch Galleries, Scottsdale, Arizona, 1994

Mackey Gallery, Denver, Colorado, 1994

Espace Timbaud, Paris, France, 1993

Small Works, Elaine Horwitch Galleries, Scottsdale, Arizona, 1993

Chicago International Art Exposition, Elaine Horwitch Gallery, Chicago, Illinois, 1992

Stremmel Gallery, Reno, Nevada, 1991

Marilyn Butler Gallery, Scottsdale, Arizona, 1990

Selected Awards

Artist Material Grant, Contemporary Forum, Phoenix, Arizona, 1991

Purchase Award, Yuma Fine Arts Center (Southwestern Invitational), Yuma, Arizona, 1989

Gallery Affiliations

Elaine Horwitch Galleries, Scottsdale, Arizona

Mackey Gallery, Denver, Colorado

Malton Gallery, Cincinnati, Ohio

Born 1960 in Cincinnati, Ohio

B.F.A., Arizona State University, Tempe, Arizona, 1984

Research Assistant, Arizona State University, Tempe, Arizona, 1984–1986

Resides in Phoenix, Arizona

KEVIN MILLER

Kevin Miller's paintings "are concerned with lost identities and fragmented selves. They look at the relationship of the individual to the whole, the means by which we are identified, how we are remembered, and how we remember others." In a series of large (approximately six-by-eight-foot) canvases, he covered the surface with fingerprints in loose grids or swirling patterns. Although from a distance the pattern predominates, each fingerprint is unique in terms of the density of paint and amount of pressure applied to the surface and also in terms of the individuality a fingerprint symbolizes. It is therefore both an abstract, formal element and the mark of an individual human being, even more characteristic than a person's name.

In other works Miller covers his canvases with newspaper obituaries or telephone book pages on which he obliterates or obscures individual names or whole sections. In contrast to the fingerprint paintings which seem life-affirming—both in the retained individuality of each print and in the implied, physical act or presence of the individual making that mark—these works seem to suggest the insignificance or vulnerability of a single life which may be reduced to a line of type and cancelled out with one stroke. "By using direct means and allowing the handmade qualities of the work to dominate, my goal is to move beyond a visual representation and to imbue these paintings with a physical presence and a genuine sense of mortality and continuity." KS

Selected Individual Exhibitions

Lost & Found, Newspace, Los Angeles, California, 1994

Selected Group Exhibitions

Current Abstractions, Municipal Art Gallery, Barnsdall Art Park, Hollywood, California, 1994

Crossing LA Home, Place, Memory, The L.A. Festival, Brand Library Art Galleries, Glendale, California, 1993

The Elegant, the Irreverent and the Obsessive, Drawing in Southern California, California State University Fullerton, Main Gallery, Fullerton, California, 1993 (Traveled to Dorothy Goldeen Gallery, Santa Monica, California)

Newspace, Los Angeles, California, 1993

Not on Canvas, Asher/Faure Gallery, Los Angeles, California, 1991

Fresh Art from Hollywood, Newspace, Los Angeles, California, 1989

Gallery Affiliation

Newspace, Los Angeles, California

Born 1956 in Santa Clara, California

B.A., Art, California State University, Long Beach, California, 1984

Resides in Los Angeles, California

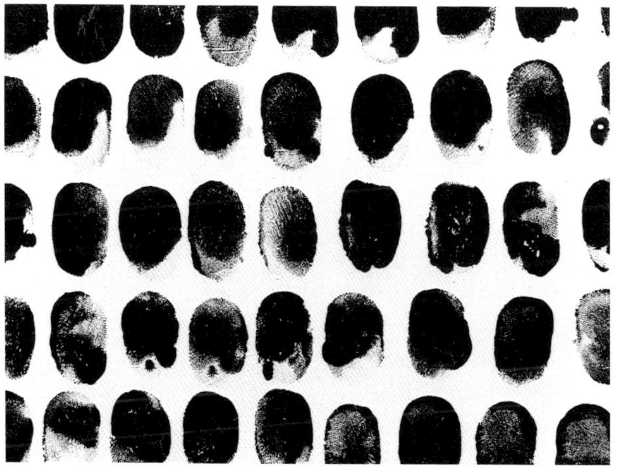

BLIND FAITH (detail), *1990*
Oil on canvas
79″ × 85″ × 3½″
Courtesy of Newspace Gallery

KENNA MOSER

For Kenna Moser the cross or cruciform is a universal symbol of "the sacredness of our relationship to nature, a link between the human and the divine." Using this symbol as a basic format for her small (usually four-by-four-inch) paintings on redwood, she adds other "symbols of nature, humanity, and spirituality" to create groupings of icon-like objects that are intended to represent our relationship to the natural world. For example, as in Relic #6, *she may paint a* milagro *of forearm and hand on one panel, overlay a handwritten text with a key on the second panel, and depict a black and white feather upon a third white panel with text, setting up layers and cross-references of images that bring them together in a unified but diverse whole. Her combination of such materials as redwood and beeswax with her texts and images of, say, an egg, leaf, or feather adds a literal dimension to her work, suggesting that the art-making process itself may provide one means of connecting with the natural world.*

Moser's tiny intimate "relics" evolve from a concern that we have become dissociated from nature and a desire to reactivate a healthier relationship with it. Thus like traditional relics or milagros, *her paintings embody both the urge to preserve something past and a faith and hope for the future.* KS

Selected Group Exhibitions

In the Spirit of Nature, San Jose Museum of Art, San Jose, California, 1994

New to the Gallery, Susan Cummins Gallery, Mill Valley, California, 1994

Nature, Gail Severn Gallery, Ketchum, Idaho, 1994

Salon Exhibition, Lee Arthur Fine Art, New York, New York, 1994

Exposure, Quo Quo Gallery, Hong Kong, 1994

Icons in Contemporary Art, California Crafts Museum, San Francisco, California, 1993

Icons, Objects, Fetishes, Studio Raid Gallery, Los Angeles, California, 1993

Radius 1993, Palo Alto Cultural Center, Palo Alto, California, 1993

In Reverence of Wood, University Art Gallery, Hayward State, California, 1993

Crocker–Kingsley Annual, Crocker Art Museum, Sacramento, California, 1993

Selected Awards

Artist Fellowship, Arts Council of Santa Clara County, San Jose, California, 1992

Gallery Affiliation

Susan Cummins Gallery, Mill Valley, California

Born 1964 in London, Ontario, Canada

B.F.A., Queens University, Kingston, Ontario, Canada, 1988

Resides in Palo Alto, California

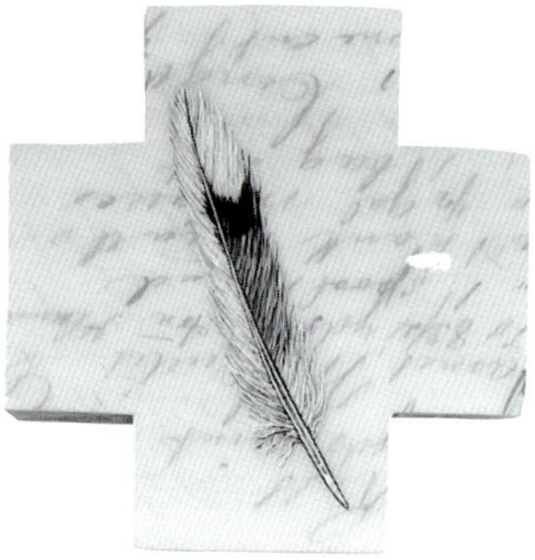

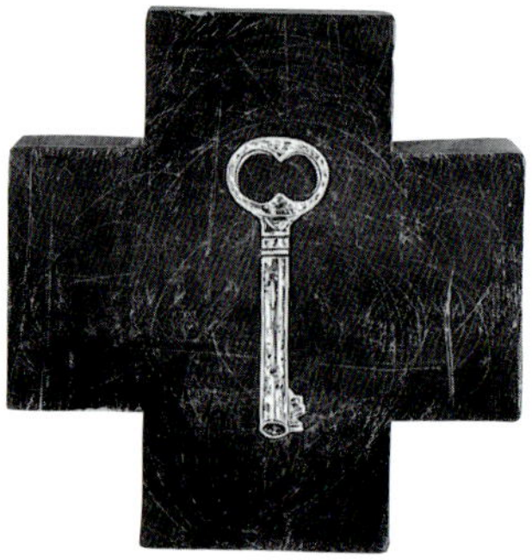

RELIC #2: FEATHER AND KEY, *1993*
Beeswax, vintage text, and oil paint on redwood
2 panels (4″ x 4″ each)
Courtesy of Susan Cummins Gallery

JEAN RASENBERGER

Through video and video installations, Jean Rasenberger explores "the collusion between narrative structures of identification and modes of projection found in the 'day to day' language of a celebrity's diary, an MTV video, a film trailer, or more specifically the fragmentation of filmic language. . ." A diaristic investigation into her own identity links her works, although while in most projects she is the actor in the tapes, she places herself in the role of another, for example, in her porno film videos and her appropriations of American photographs of the nude. In the humorous, ironic, and self-deprecating style of Cindy Sherman, Rasenberger tries these images on for size, substituting herself for the heroine of a pulp film or as the subject of Eleanor, Chicago, 1949, *a Harry Callahan photograph.*

Through this strategy, she also reveals normally unrecognized cinematic conventions. By removing the erotic content of a porno film, for instance, she may point to its essential vacuity, undermining its effective authority and disclosing its absurdity. "My work is concerned with locating structures of what I call 'filler,' like the space found in the narratives of porno films, or the 'filler' that surrounds an object of attention. This is a space of indeterminate familiarity, a space in which identification is sought, or saturated, and projection is frustrated, or overloaded." KS

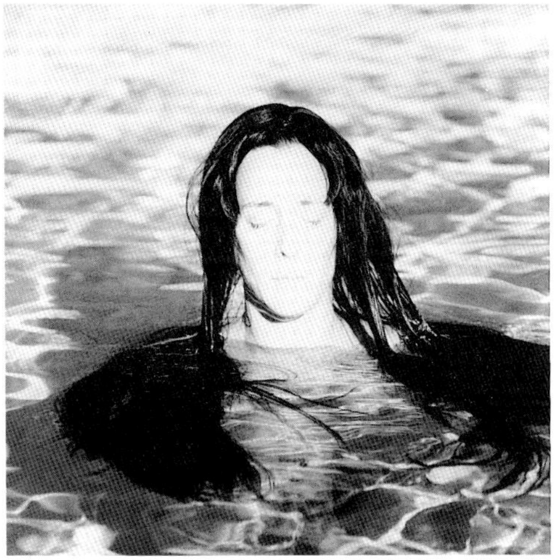

UNTITLED (Eleanor), *1994*
Black and white laser print
52" × 52"

Selected Individual Exhibitions

University of California, Riverside, University Art Gallery, Riverside, California, 1994

Selected Group Exhibitions

When Worlds Collide, Museum of Modern Art, New York, New York, 1994

[Cut] Los Angeles/90'ERNES Kunstscene, Kunstforeningen, Copenhagen, Denmark, and Gallery F 15, Moss, Norway, 1994

Three Solo Performances, Rosamund Felsen Gallery, Los Angeles, California, and Lace, Hollywood, California, 1994

Sampler: Southern California Videotape Collection, Studio Guenzani, Milan, Italy, 1994

Sugar and Spice, Long Beach Museum of Art, Long Beach, California, 1993

From Without, The Apartment, Los Angeles, California, 1993

Selected Awards

Brody Arts Fund Fellowship, California Community Foundation, Los Angeles, California, 1994

Open Channels Grant, Long Beach Museum of Art, Long Beach, California, 1992

Born 1959 in Washington, District of Columbia

M.F.A., Art Center College of Design, Pasadena, California, 1992

B.A., Sarah Lawrence College, Bronxville, New York, 1982

Studio Art, Whitney Museum of Independent Study Program, New York, New York, 1983

Resides in Los Angeles, California

RIGO 94

Rigo 94 borrows from advertising/ propaganda strategies and imagery to create installations and paintings that call attention to consumer society's means for influencing our desires and viewpoints. Using a signpainter's graphic style, a limited palette (often just red, black, and white), and bold, blocky text, he produces works reminiscent of the billboards, corporate logos, and advertisement that bombard us every day. However, Rigo 94's juxtapositions of text and imagery are intended to introduce an element of doubt into our reading. For example, an eight-by-thirty-foot acrylic on canvas depicting a sleek red sportscar and a hand-held pack of cigarettes is captioned by the title Hooked on Despair, *alluding to the automobile and tobacco industries' dependence on the consumer's desires for and/or addictions to their products. In his installation titled* Adprop-one dream come two, *Rigo 94 incorporated a floor painted like a parking lot and sign-like paintings with such texts as: "After these first 500 years of success, nothing like sitting back and enjoying a long failure" and "Now more than ever we believe in the strength of your convictions."*

Other works reveal often negative social stereotypes that pervade consumer culture, in particular his series of push-pin images and portraits that pair references to Native Americans with an automobile name (Jeep) *or weapon* (Missile), *again prompting us to reexamine many of the insidious messages we unconsciously consume every day.* KS

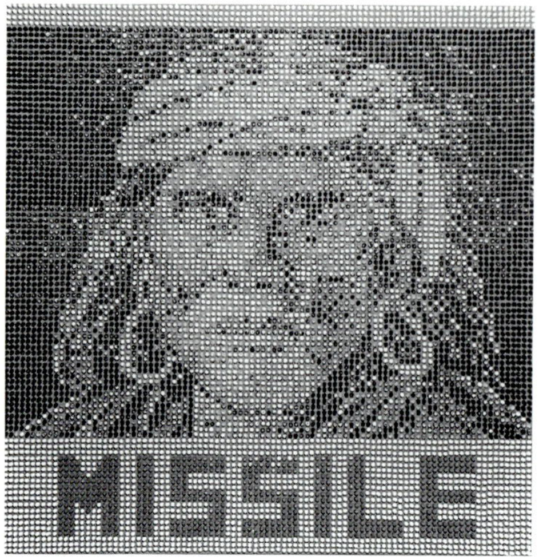

MISSILE, *1992*
Pushpins on wood
48" x 48"
Collection of Ren Di Rosa

Selected Individual Exhibitions

Eagles, The Lab Gallery, San Francisco, California, 1994

Westward, The Living Room, San Francisco, California, 1994

Largo Do Canto Do Muro, Galeria Porta 33, Funchal, Portugal, 1994

Adprop-one dream come two, Southern Exposure Gallery, San Francisco, California, 1992

Selected Group Exhibitions

20th Anniversary Alumni Exhibition, Southern Exposure Gallery, San Francisco, California, 1994

Trespassing, LACE/Los Angeles Contemporary Exhibitions, Los Angeles, California, 1992

Introductions, Gallery Paule Anglim, San Francisco, California, 1992

RIGO 91/Scott Williams, Show 'n' Tell Gallery, San Francisco, California, 1991

Selected Awards

Art in the Urban Landscape, Capp Street Project, San Francisco, California, 1994

Artist-in-Residence, California Arts Council, San Francisco, California, 1992–1994

LUSO, American Development Foundation Grant, Lisbon, Portugal, 1992

Gallery Affiliation

Gallery Paule Anglim, San Francisco, California

Born 1966 in Madeira Island, Portugal

B.F.A., Performance/Video, San Francisco Art Institute, San Francisco, California, 1991

Resides in San Francisco, California

SARA ROBERTS

For eight years Sara Roberts has been working with interactive video installations, "making portraits of common relationships: Mother and child; watcher and watched; person and thing; husband, wife, and friends. In these installations video and physical space work together to establish tensions which involve the visitor in a kind of social sculpture. . . . The visitor participates as a whole person, not just with eyes and mind." Roberts' user-friendly approach to video illustrates a humanist goal for today's technology, and her choice of subjects indicates her interest in reinforcing an emotional and physical involvement with her art despite its high-tech medium.

In Early Programming, *for example, Roberts creates the familiar situation of sitting at the kitchen table with Mom. But this Mom is a computer named MARGO with a monotone machine voice that responds with such typical quips as "Because I say you have to!" MARGO also has an on-screen rectangle that conveys a sterner "mood" by getting smaller and darker. Roberts' basis for* Digital Museum *was "the contemporary shift in emphasis from finding, naming, and categorizing to seeking the relationships between that which has been collected and ourselves questioning objectivity." Through this piece she explores the primary relationship of touch, making a finger that reaches through a glass to touch each object the "digit" rather than the mathematical digit of computer technology.*
KS

Selected Individual Exhibitions

Elective Affinities, Yerba Buena Center for the Arts, San Francisco, California, 1994

Selected Group Exhibitions

A New Sensation, Interactive Gallery, Moscone Center, Seybold '93, San Francisco, California, 1993

Iterations, International Center for Photography, New York, New York, 1993

Iterations, Montage '93, Rochester, New York, 1993

The Territories, Contemporary Art Museum of Chicago, Chicago, Illinois, 1992

Images du Futur, Cite des Arts et des Nouvelles Technologies du Montreal, Montreal, Quebec, Canada, 1991

Mother and Child Reunion, Long Beach Museum of Art, Long Beach, California, 1990

Tableaux Vivants, San Francisco Arts Commission Gallery, San Francisco, California, 1989

Selected Awards

Residency, Djerassi Foundation, Woodside, California, 1993

Award of Merit, Ford Foundation, New York, New York, 1979

Born 1955 in Milwaukee, Wisconsin

M.F.A., Film/Video, California College of Arts and Crafts, Oakland, California, 1988

B.A., Art, Western Washington University, Bellingham, Washington, 1978

Resides in Emeryville, California

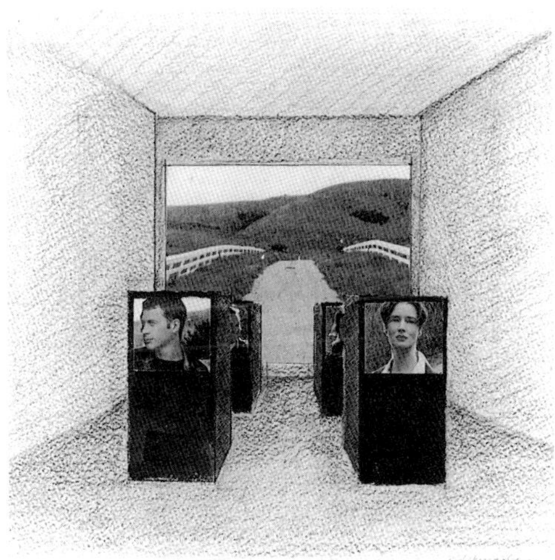

ELECTIVE AFFINITIES (work in progress)
Mixed/electronic media
2 rooms: 15′ × 15′ and 10′ × 10′
Sketch: Donna Schumacher

JOSÉ LUIS RODRÍGUEZ

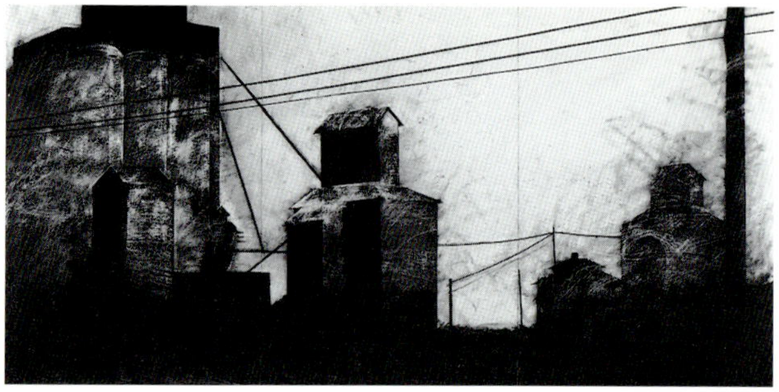

Gothic, *1992*
Charcoal on paper
44″ x 90″

Dark, looming silhouettes of factories and mills fill José Luis Rodríguez's large charcoal drawings. Smudged with charcoal dust, like the buildings they depict might be, the images are dense and layered, built up over time. The works executed in wax and colored pigments, for example Tower *or* Anchor, *are more abstract but nonetheless convey a mysterious, monolithic presence that is strangely romantic. Rodríguez's titles as well suggest this mood:* Gothic, Citadel, *and* Mausoleo *all refer to architectural structures of another time and place or of a more monumental function.*

A certain nostalgia pervades Rodríguez's works. The structures he portrays generally seem stilled, vacant, fallen into disuse. There is no human activity evident except in his own gestural markings that seem as much a part of his process of interacting with his materials as of capturing a mood or quality of his subject. Yet within that activity of markmaking may lie the essence of his work: "I am trying to express my relationship to structures that surround me. I'm particularly interested in what I perceive as visual remnants of an Industrial Age and the kind of subtle impression it now maintains. My aim is not to be confrontational with these pieces but to somehow acquire a sense of how surrounded we are by structures that mark our progress historically." Rodríguez's marks themselves may be seen as the remnants or by-products of his own relationship with the process of building a drawing. *KS*

Selected Individual Exhibitions

José L. Rodríguez, Obras Sobre Papel, Centro de Bellas Artes, Maracaibo, Venezuela, 1992

José L. Rodríguez, Cafe Gallery, Albuquerque, New Mexico, 1992

José L. Rodríguez, West Texas State University, Canyon, Texas, 1991

Focus on Faculty, José L. Rodríguez, University of New Mexico Art Museum, Albuquerque, New Mexico, 1990

Selected Group Exhibitions

Hand Pulled Prints, Blue Star, San Antonio, Texas, 1994

Sporting Life, Nabisco Gallery, Hanover, New Jersey, 1994

9th Annual National Works on Paper, University of Texas, Tyler, Texas, 1994

Works on Paper, Cafe Gallery, Albuquerque, New Mexico, 1993

UNM Printmaking, Universidad de las Americas, Cholula, Mexico, 1993

Group Exhibition, Freites-Revilla Gallery, Boca Raton, Florida, 1992

Selected Awards

Purchase Award, 9th Annual National Works on Paper, University of Texas, Tyler, Texas, 1994

College of Fine Arts Research Grant, University of New Mexico, Albuquerque, New Mexico, 1992

Jurors Award, Harper College Print & Drawing Exhibition, Palatine, Illinois, 1990

Gallery Affiliations

Cafe Gallery, Albuquerque, New Mexico

Freites-Revilla Gallery, Boca Raton, Florida

Born 1959 in Maracaibo, Venezuela

M.F.A., Indiana University, Bloomington, Indiana, 1987

B.F.A., University of Oklahoma, Norman, Oklahoma, 1983

Industrial Design, Apprenticeship, Siemens A.G., Munich, Germany, 1981

Resides in Albuquerque, New Mexico

GREGORY SCHULTE

Working in the age-old traditions of still life and realism, Gregory Schulte renders in careful detail with graphite such found objects as bones, dead fish, dried plants, and sometimes instruments like a compass or pencil. Taped, nailed, or strung up on a textured background—usually a piece of unfolded old paper or cloth—the objects seem to take on significance simply by virtue of their having been discovered, displayed, and transformed by his meticulous observation and articulation. Often these objects are characterized by weathering, aging, decomposition, or the accumulation of matter. Schulte renders them "with a heightened awareness of surface detail and texture to underscore the central concept that all things are in a continuous and varying state of change due to natural processes and human modification."

Most of these objects also have some personal meaning for Schulte, whether due to a particular experience he associates with them or just because of a certain physical aspect that attracts him. Some, like the bone fragment in Sacred Sacrum, *bound along a geometric configuration of twine, look as though they might even carry some ritualistic symbolism. Yet Schulte's works also have the direct, unassuming quality of sheerly formal studies, drawn and viewed for the pleasure and exercise of looking and discovering the richness of apparently simple things.* KS

Selected Individual Exhibitions

Gregory Schulte—Recent Work, Grace Chosy Gallery, Madison, Wisconsin, 1992

Selected Group Exhibitions

Landscape & Still Life, Comus Gallery, Portland, Oregon, 1994

Eighteenth Annual National Invitational Drawing Exhibition, Emporia State University, Norman R. Eppink Art Gallery, Emporia, Kansas, 1994

37th Chautauqua National Exhibition of American Art, Chautauqua Institution, Chautauqua Art Association Gallery, Chautauqua, New York, 1994

24th Bradley National Print & Drawing Exhibition, Bradley University, Hartmann & Heuser Galleries, Peoria, Illinois, 1993

Drawing 1993, Brigham Young University, Harris Fine Arts Center, Provo, Utah, 1993

American Realism Competition, Parkersburg Art Center, Parkersburg, West Virginia, 1992

6th Annual Greater Midwest International, Central Missouri State University, Warrensburg, Missouri, 1991

Selected Awards

Purchase Award, 24th Bradley National Print & Drawing Exhibition, Peoria, Illinois, 1993

Faculty Research Grant, Utah State University, Logan, Utah, 1993

First Place (drawing), Breckenridge Fine Arts Center National Juried Competition, Breckenridge, Texas, 1993

Gallery Affiliations

Comus Gallery, Portland, Oregon

Grace Chosy Gallery, Madison, Wisconsin

Born 1964 in Stuttgart, Germany

M.F.A., University of Wisconsin, Madison, Wisconsin, 1991

B.F.A., University of Wisconsin, Madison, Wisconsin, 1987

Resides in Logan, Utah

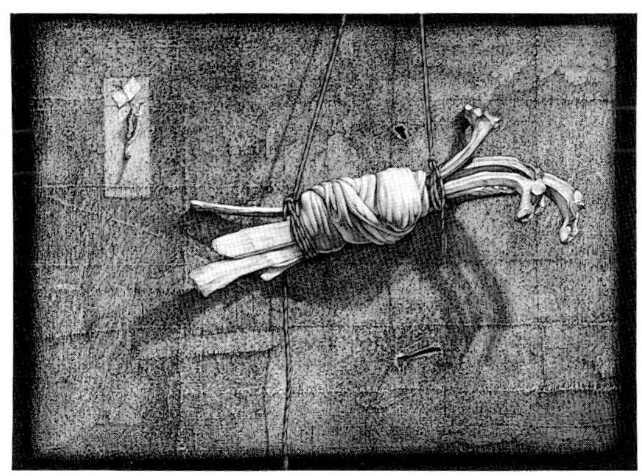

FRAMED REMAINS, *1994*
Graphite and gesso on paper
21" x 28"

PAT WARING SHERWOOD

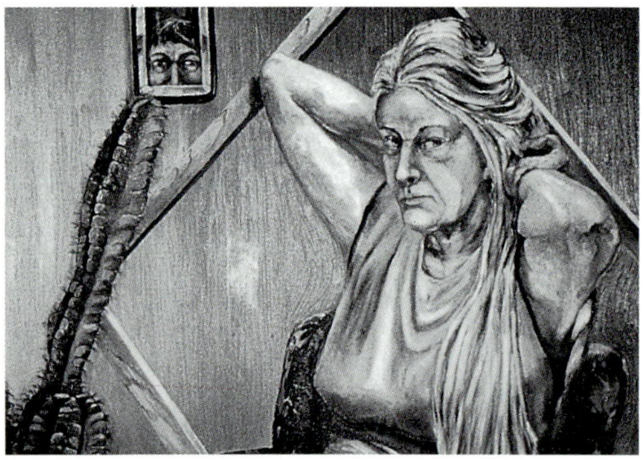

REMEMBERING ARIZONA
(detail), *1994*
Oil on canvas
36" x 36"

For Pat Waring Sherwood painting seems to be an act of straightforward communication, a means of sharing with others what she has endured and felt as a middle-aged woman: "The often quoted phrase 'the invisible woman' (those about, or over, forty) is a sad truth. My paintings are about the loneliness of aging in this youth-oriented society. I paint what I know and have experienced, i.e., divorce, isolation (invisibleness), financial difficulties, problems regarding body image." Her style is direct, emphasizing content over virtuosity, and reflecting her unidealized acceptance of life. Her images are candid portraits that convey a vulnerable yet courageous (and at times humorous) stance with regard to her and others' circumstance. Through them, Sherwood hopes not only to represent her own experiences but "to reach people, to have someone say, 'Yes, I have felt that; I recognize that.'"

Christmas Dinner *is a poignant scene in which a woman sits at her kitchen table eating take-out food, her suitcase at hand as though it had been packed in hopes of an invitation to a more cheerful celebration. The perspective places us in a position of looking down somewhat at the seated woman, making her seem even more pitiable. Yet her gaze confronts us; despite having caught her in this humiliating situation, she seems unabashed, almost defiant. The strength and resolution in her eyes are like a gift to the rest of us.* KS

Selected Individual Exhibitions

Pat Sherwood—New Paintings, Mission College, Santa Clara, California, 1993

Pat Sherwood—Paintings, Faculty Club, Stanford University, Stanford, California, 1993

Pat Sherwood—Paintings, Los Gatos Museum, Los Gatos, California, 1992

Pat Sherwood—Prints, Palo Alto Cultural Center, Palo Alto, California, 1977

Pat Sherwood—Painter, RayChem Corporation, Sunnyvale, California, 1969

Pat Sherwood—Painter, Triton Museum, Santa Clara, California, 1968

Selected Group Exhibitions

California Society of Printmakers, San Jose Museum, San Jose, California, 1976

Bay Area Graphics, De Anza College, Euphrat Gallery, Cupertino, California, 1975

Women Artists, Oakland Museum, Oakland, California, 1969

Artists of the West, Charles & Emma Frye Museum, Seattle, Washington, 1968

Selected Awards

Purchase, Mills College, Oakland, California, 1978

Purchase, Bank of America, San Francisco, California, 1977

First-Painting, Art Educators, Lytton Center, Palo Alto, California, 1968

Born 1933 in Columbia, South Carolina

M.F.A., Mills College, Oakland, California, 1974

B.F.A., California State University, Hayward, California, 1970

Printmaking, Artist-in-Residence, Centrum Frans Masereel, Kasterlee, Belgium, 1989

Graduate School, Art, San Jose State University, San Jose, California, 1970–1972

Painting, Boston Museum School of Fine Arts, Boston, Massachusetts, 1950–1952

Resides in Los Altos, California

CHRISTOPHER T. TERRY

Christopher Terry's interiors and still lifes have a quiet, almost eerie sense about them, as though something had just happened or were about to happen—perhaps like an empty stage set. And like a stage set, they are created to look real but do not necessarily reproduce an actual time and place: "The subject of my paintings, although based in reality, is more often invented than drawn from direct observation . . . By working from my imagination instead of an objective reality, the images become more meditative or dreamlike in quality." Indeed, his images seem almost translucent as though created by light instead of paint, giving them an ethereal, transitory character.

Yet the sensuousness of his subjects is also present. Focusing on surface textures, particularly walls and drapery, Terry may combine tables, shelves, empty frames, and architectural details in compositions that are almost abstract in their play of ordered geometry against the disorganized patterns of folds and wrinkles in the fabric. Terry thinks of the surfaces of the fabric and walls as "skin-like" and the interiors they occupy as "ritual environments." As such his paintings may be seen as metaphors for how one inhabits the world. Even though there are no actual figures in them, they appeal to our sense of touch and physical experience with the objects that surround us. *KS*

Selected Individual Exhibitions

Recent Paintings, Contemporary Realist Gallery, San Francisco, California, 1993

Cerro Coso Community College, Ridgecrest, California, 1992

Atrium Gallery, Salt Lake City, Utah, 1992

New Paintings, Nora Eccles Harrison Museum of Art, Logan, Utah, 1991

New Still Lifes, Contemporary Realist Gallery, San Francisco, California, 1989

New Work, Contemporary Realist Gallery, San Francisco, California, 1987

Paintings, Contemporary Realist Gallery, San Francisco, California, 1986

Selected Group Exhibitions

Cheekwood National, The Cheekwood Museum of Art, Nashville, Tennessee, 1993

New American Talent, Laguna Gloria Museum, Austin, Texas, 1992

Selected Awards

Fulbright Scholar Award, Council for International Exchange of Scholars, Washington, District of Columbia, 1994

Best in Show, Charlotte International, Charlotte, North Carolina, 1993

Visual Artist Fellowship, Utah Arts Council, Salt Lake City, Utah, 1990

Gallery Affiliations

Contemporary Realist Gallery, San Francisco, California

John Thomas Gallery, Los Angeles, California

Born 1956 in Stamford, Connecticut

M.F.A., Painting, University of Wisconsin, Madison, Wisconsin, 1981

B.A., Studio Art, Rhode Island College, Providence, Rhode Island, 1978

Resides in Logan, Utah

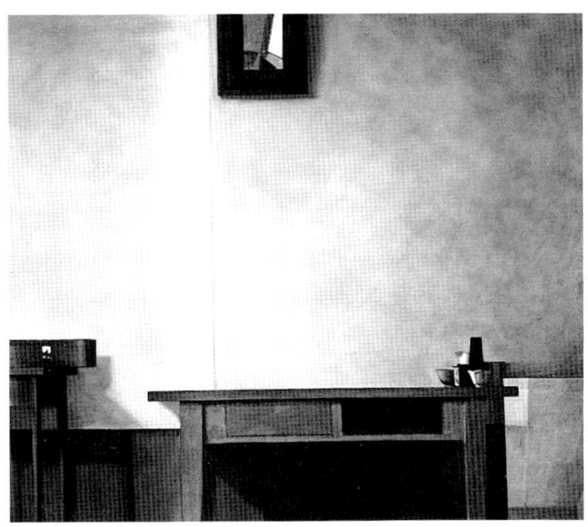

DULCIMER CASE, *1992*
Oil on canvas
36" x 42"

EV THOMAS

Huge solitary boulders and shapes of land and water dominate Ev Thomas' often monumentally scaled paintings. Painted roughly and heavily—they sometimes take months, even years, to complete—they seem to have the texture of stone itself. Even their palette, which is all muted grays, browns, and a little blue, scumbled and built up over time, is like that of granite or shale. In most works the water, sky, and land, and any rock or road in it, almost fuse together into an overall patterning of light and shade and subtle variations in surface. Suggestive of the harsh, gray, desolate landscapes of Wales or Easter Island, they could just as well be Thomas' interpretation of almost any place or they may even be landscapes partially or wholly created in his mind.

Although his compositions exclude the human figure, Thomas' paintings speak of a human relationship with nature, one that may be melancholy and alienating or awestruck and sublime: "My work is a painterly and personal dialogue with elements of the landscape around me . . . dirt, water, rock. I am trying to make a simplified and symbolic picture of the elemental forces as represented by the earth. I do not mean any of this abstractly. These paintings are a personal expression of faith in the importance of the land to the psyche and to the culture." KS

Selected Individual Exhibitions

Monte Clark Gallery, Vancouver, British Columbia, Canada, 1993

Walker and Walker Gallery, Santa Monica, California, 1990

Mincher Wilcox Gallery, San Francisco, California, 1988

SECA Award, San Francisco Museum of Modern Art, San Francisco, California, 1986

Khiva Gallery, San Francisco, California, 1985

Selected Group Exhibitions

Cadavre Exquis, Drawing Center, New York, New York, 1993

Larry Evans Fine Art, San Francisco, California, 1993

Sara Rentschler Gallery, New York, New York, 1985

Triangle Gallery, San Francisco, California, 1980

San Francisco Arts Commission Gallery, San Francisco, California, 1979

Selected Awards

Pollock—Krasner Foundation Grant, New York, New York, 1993

Individual Artist Support Award for Painting, Marin County Arts Council, San Rafael, California, 1992

Society for the Encouragement of Contemporary Art (SECA), San Francisco Museum of Modern Art, San Francisco, California, 1986

Gallery Affiliations

Larry Evans Fine Art, San Francisco, California

Monte Clark Gallery, Vancouver, British Columbia, Canada

Born 1949 in Danville, Illinois

B.A., Southern Illinois University, Carbondale, Illinois, 1972

Resides in Bolinas, California

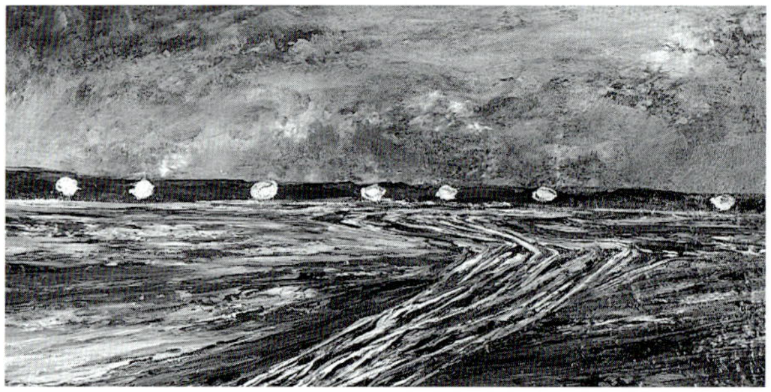

UFORIA, *1993*
Oil on canvas
8" × 16¾"

CANAN TOLON

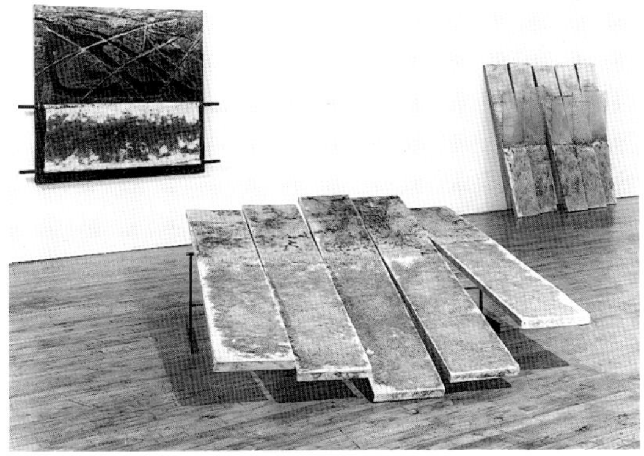

SEESAW LANDSCAPE
(center structure of an installation view), *1993*
Acrylic on canvas, with wood, steel, weights, coffee grounds, garment patterns, grass seeds, and grass
24″ x 72″ x 78″

Although Canan Tolon uses acrylic on canvas, she also incorporates other materials such as grass, coffee grounds, plexiglas, metal, and wood into her "paintings." In some works she actually grows grass on canvas, letting it die and change colors over the course of an exhibition. Or, she may make "machines which produce 'drawings' and 'paintings' on canvas by means of a variety of processes such as staining, (grass) growth, wear, rot, etc." She also may juxtapose a painted landscape with maps and surveying diagrams in order to "represent an environment in a transitional state of construction and destruction."

Rather than simply represent her concern for the landscape and nature through painted images that allow us to keep the issues at a physical and psychological distance, Tolon's mixed media works literally bring them into the gallery and into our own space. Her series of "Still Lifes" (an ironic use of the art-historical term since they include real grasses that are growing or have died) lean against the wall, and their industrial-like structures project into the room. The juxtaposition of beautifully painted landscapes with human-made grid elements overlaying them actualizes what Tolon considers to be our mechanized "conquering" of nature. *KS*

Selected Individual Exhibitions

Still Lifes, Center for Contemporary Art, Santa Fe, New Mexico, 1993

Baski, Galeri Nev, Istanbul, Turkey, 1993

Introductions, Harcourts Modern and Contemporary Art Gallery, San Francisco, California, 1992

Landscapes, Pro-Arts Gallery, Oakland, California, 1991

Still Lifes, University of California, Berkeley, California, 1990

Selected Group Exhibitions

Coming Across, De Anza College, Euphrat Museum of Art, Cupertino, California, 1994

Contemporary Women Artists, Topkapi Museum, Istanbul, Turkey, 1993

Istanbul International Biennial, Istanbul, Turkey, 1992

Re-Generation, San Jose Art Institute, San Jose, California, 1992

Off the Wall, Sheldon Memorial Art Museum, Lincoln, Nebraska, 1991

Born 1955 in Istanbul, Turkey

M.A., Architecture, University of California, Berkeley, California, 1993

B.A., Middlesex Polytecnic, London, England, 1980

Resides in Berkeley, California

TRIMPIN

Trimpin's work is "an ongoing exploration of the concepts of sound, vision, and movement, experimenting with combinations that will introduce our senses of perception to a totally new experience. Although I use the latest technology available, I work with 'natural' elements—water, air, light, etc.—and reconfigure them in new and unusual applications, pushing them to the limits, and beyond, of what we traditionally think of as their role."

In Liquid Percussion *Trimpin uses an array of mostly handblown glass vessels as "instruments" which are finely tuned to produce specific sounds and timbres when struck by "rainfall"—falling waterdrops controlled manually or by a special keyboard through a complex valve system suspended from the ceiling. In* Phffft-Arrrgh *he combines nearly 200 computer-controlled wind instruments—brass horns, whistles, organ pipes, flutes, accordion reeds, etc.—in a mechanized choreography of sound in space. Although computerized, the entire installation is air-activated and acoustic, drawing upon the most ancient and natural medium of musical and verbal articulation. Thus Trimpin's elaborate, custom-designed, mechanical "instruments" are always the physical means to a musical or audible end; while they add a visual and sculptural dimension to his sound installations, they are only secondary to his pursuit of a harmonious interaction of nature and technology and an expansive new experience of sound.* KS

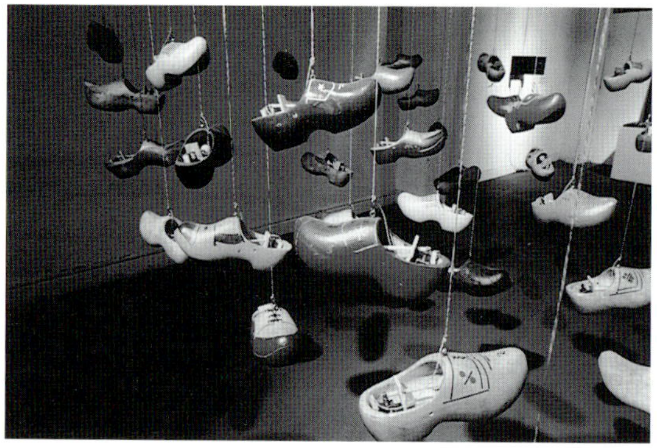

HANGING KLOMPEN, *1991*
Music sculpture
15′ x 30′ x 30′

Selected Individual Installations/ Performances

Phffft, New York Philharmonic, Lincoln Center, New York, 1994

Phffft, Tacoma Art Museum, Tacoma, Washington, 1994

Palacio Bellas Artes, Mexico City, Mexico, 1993

Suspended Sound Illusions, New Langton Arts, San Francisco, California, 1991

Liquid Percussion, Museum Technorama, Winterthur, Switzerland, 1991

Floating Klompen, Jan van Eyck Arts Academy, Maastrich, Holland, 1987

Ringo, Stedelijk Modern Art Museum, Amsterdam, Holland, 1986

Selected Group Installations/ Performances

Ringo, Arte Virtual, Madrid, Spain, 1994

IPP71512, The Kitchen, New York, New York, 1993

London, Sound Symposium, Newfoundland, Canada, 1992

Cocktails, Banff Art Center, Banff, Canada, 1990

Selected Awards

Grant, Seattle Arts Commission, Seattle, Washington, 1993

NEA Grant, Washington, District of Columbia, 1992

Grant, Art Matters, New York, New York, 1989

Born 1951 in Istein, Germany

Social Studies, University of Berlin, Berlin, Germany, 1976

Music Theory/Composition, University of Berlin, Berlin, Germany, 1979

Mechanical Engineering, Freiburg, Germany, 1969

Resides in Seattle, Washington

FAN WARREN

Fan Warren's "Middle Passage" series depicts images of "structural buildings which are both tables and thrones in West African culture. They are utilitarian objects that hold and contain yet are symbols of power." Made from materials found in her environment, the images are also about her "everyday reality; references to the process of living in the present that has been shaped by the past; symbolic of how the future is being constructed by what is taking place daily." For Warren, "they are housing the souls and memories of my identity as a Black American," providing a personal connection with her own cultural past and future.

Painted or drawn on old crumpled pieces of paper, ranging in size from 8 by 6 inches to 63 by 48 inches, the solitary table-like objects are most often rendered in black and white with muted background colors. Although drawn in perspective (at times exaggerated), they float in an ambiguous space, accentuating the disparity between two and three dimensions. The works themselves, however, with their ragged edges and crinkled surfaces or contained as some are in a frame (a found object), reassert their physical presence. As such they have the feel of a Byzantine icon or a Mexican retablo, *embodying and invoking the power of revered images through the materials of daily life.* KS

Selected Individual Exhibitions

Fan Warren, Paintings, Isobel Neal Gallery, Chicago, Illinois, 1992

In the Middle Passage, Artemisia Gallery, Chicago, Illinois, 1991

Selected Group Exhibitions

Borders and Boundaries, Spertus Museum, Chicago, Illinois, 1994

Home Girls, Beacon Street Gallery, Chicago, Illinois, 1994

Like That There, C.A.G.E. Gallery, Cincinnati, Ohio, 1992

The Legacy of Africa, I.T.N.W., Waterloo Museum of Art, Davenport, Iowa, 1991

Roots an Extension, State of Illinois Gallery, Chicago, Illinois, 1988

Detroit Focus, Detroit Gallery, Detroit, Michigan, 1987

Installations, Artemisia Gallery, Chicago, Illinois, 1987

Selected Awards

City of Chicago, Department of Cultural Affairs, CAA Grant, Chicago, Illinois, 1991

City of Chicago, Department of Cultural Affairs, CAA Grant, Chicago, Illinois, 1989

Illinois State University, Elizabeth Stein Scholarship, Normal, Illinois, 1982

Gallery Affiliations

Isobel Neal Gallery, Chicago, Illinois

Born 1957 in Birmingham, Alabama

M.F.A., School of the Art Institute, Chicago, Illinois, 1985

B.F.A., Illinois State University, Normal, Illinois, 1982

Curatorial Research Assistant, Museum of Contemporary Art, Chicago, Illinois, 1983–1985

Resides in Oakland, California

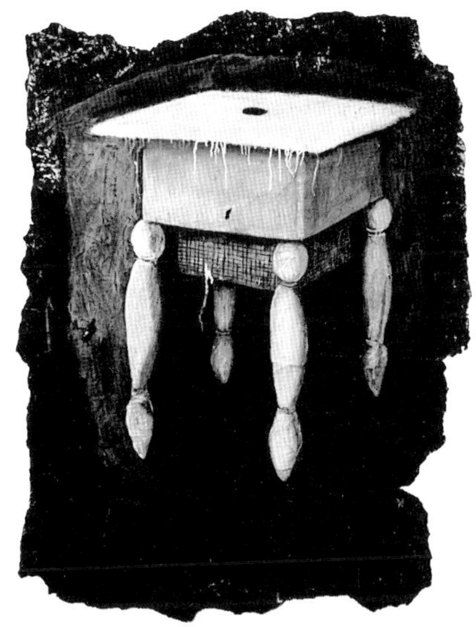

BLACK TRAPPER, *1991*
Mixed media, 40″ × 53″
Courtesy of Isobel Neal Gallery

1994 AWARDS AND HONORABLE MENTIONS

PAINTING RECIPIENTS

Dennis L. Angel
Henderson, Nevada

Maura Bendett
Los Angeles, California

Sandow Birk
Los Angeles, California

Cristina Cardenas
Tucson, Arizona

Susan Kelk Cervantes
San Francisco, California

Dorothy A. Faison
Kailua, Hawaii

Kay French
Portland, Oregon

Paul Green
Portland, Oregon

Diane Andrews Hall
San Francisco, California

Michael Marlowe
Phoenix, Arizona

Kevin Miller
Los Angeles, California

Kenna Moser
Palo Alto, California

Rigo 94
San Francisco, California

Pat Waring Sherwood
Los Altos, California

Christopher T. Terry
Logan, Utah

Ev Thomas
Bolinas, California

Canan Tolon
Berkeley, California

PAINTING ALTERNATES

Inez Storer
Inverness, California

Darren R. Waterson
Los Angeles, California

Michael Wood
Santa Fe, New Mexico

PAINTING HONORABLE MENTIONS

Victoria Adams
Vashon, Washington

Amy Crehore
Eugene, Oregon

Brad Durham
Los Angeles, California

Holly Lane
Sunnyvale, California

Kevin Sloan
Oakland, California

Vince Smith
Del Mar, California

Vicki Teague-Cooper
Santa Fe, New Mexico

NEW GENRES RECIPIENTS

James L. Acord
Richland, Washington

Jean Rasenberger
Los Angeles, California

Sara Roberts
Fmeryville, California

Trimpin
Seattle, Washington

Cinthea Fiss
Berkeley, California

NEW GENRES ALTERNATES

Ronald Lee Athey
Los Angeles, California

Susan Kornfeld
Los Angeles, California

John Wilson White
San Francisco, California

NEW GENRES HONORABLE MENTIONS

Warner Blake
Seattle, Washington

James Green
Denver, Colorado

Miira Ojanen
West Hollywood, California

Badchi Zhang
Woodland, California

Jim Campbell
San Francisco, California

Thomas Jacobs
Seattle, Washington

D. A. Therrien
Phoenix, Arizona

WORKS ON PAPER RECIPIENTS

Timothy C. Ely
Portland, Oregon

Stephen P. Hayes
Portland, Oregon

Susan Magnus
Emeryville, California

Gregory Schulte
Logan, Utah

David Green
Seattle, Washington

Deborah F. Lawrence
Seattle, Washington

José Luis Rodríguez
Albuquerque, New Mexico

Fan Warren
Oakland, California

WORKS ON PAPER ALTERNATES

Rod Appleton
Seattle, Washington

Alistair Milne
Los Angeles, California

Yoshiko Shimano
Berkeley, California

WORKS ON PAPER HONORABLE MENTIONS

Richard Bartow
South Beach, Oregon

Robin McCloskey
Palo Alto, California

Andrea Schwartz-Feit
Portland, Oregon

Kristine Spindler-Gunnell
Logan, Utah

Jane Motko Emens
San Francisco, California

ORGANIZATIONAL SUPPORT FOR CONTEMPORARY ART

The Organizational Support for Contemporary Art component of the WESTAF/NEA Regional Fellowships for Visual Artists is designed to expand the profile of the fellowship recipients. Museums, art centers, and alternative spaces throughout the United States may apply for matching grants to exhibit the work of fellowship recipients, commission new work, or develop educational activities such as in-depth residencies, workshops, and seminars. Since the program began in 1988, WESTAF has assisted more than 47 exhibitions of fellowship artists' work.

Nonprofit organizations may apply for support in presenting any artist who has received a fellowship from WESTAF since 1988. Up to $1,000 per fellowship artist is available. Organizations are eligible for support of one project in each funding cycle but may involve more than one fellowship artist in the activity.

The following factors are considered in the review of applications:

— Quality and scope of the proposed activity
— Potential benefit to the career of the fellowship artist(s), including broadest possible exposure of the artwork
— Community access to the artist and the artwork.

For more information on Organizational Support for Contemporary Art, please contact: WESTAF, 236 Montezuma Avenue, Santa Fe NM 87501; 505/988-1166; 505/982-9307 (fax); 505/988-5278 (TDD).

PREVIOUS RECIPIENTS OF ORGANIZATIONAL SUPPORT FOR CONTEMPORARY ART

Arizona State University Art Museum
Tempe AZ

Bakersfield Museum of Art
Bakersfield CA

Boise Art Museum
Boise ID

Brandywine Graphic Workshop, Inc.
Philadelphia PA

California College of Arts and Crafts
Oakland CA

California State University
Fullerton CA

Carbon County Arts Guild
Red Lodge MT

College of Santa Fe
Santa Fe NM

Cunningham Memorial Art Gallery
Bakersfield CA

Dinnerware Artists' Cooperative Gallery
Tucson AZ

Galleries of the Claremont Colleges
Claremont CA

Holter Museum of Art
Helena MT

Intersection for the Arts
San Francisco CA

La Raza/Galeria Posada
Sacramento CA

Maude Kerns Arts Center
Eugene OR

Missoula Museum of the Arts
Missoula MT

Nevada Museum of Art
Reno NV

Nicolaysen Art Museum
Casper WY

Oregon School of Arts and Crafts
Portland OR

Paris Gibson Square Museum of Art
Great Falls MT

Port Angeles Fine Arts Center
Port Angeles WA

Pritchard Art Gallery
Moscow ID

Salt Lake Art Center
Salt Lake City UT

San Francisco Camerawork
San Francisco CA

Sangre de Cristo Arts and Conference Center
Pueblo CO

Seattle Art Museum
Seattle WA

Steamboat Springs Arts Council
Steamboat Springs CO

Sushi, Inc.
San Diego CA

Tempe Arts Center
Tempe AZ

Truckee Meadows Community College
Reno NV

University Art Museum
Long Beach CA

University of California, Berkeley
Berkeley CA

Vermont Studio Center
Johnson VT

Washington State University
Pullman WA

Western Nevada Community College
Carson City NV

Whatcom Museum
Bellingham WA

XS Gallery
Carson City NV

Yellowstone Arts Center
Billings MT

HISTORY OF THE FELLOWS, 1988–1993

Seyed Alavi
Sculpture, 1993

Danaë Anderson
Crafts, 1989

Don Gregorio Antón
Photography, 1993

Anthony J. Aziz
Photography, 1991

Zhao Baiwei
Works on Paper, 1992

Kaucyila Brooke
Photography, 1991

Joy Broom
Works on Paper, 1992

Michael F. Brophy
Painting, 1990

Beliz Brother
Sculpture, 1993

Chad Buck
Works on Paper, 1988

Mark A. Calderon
Sculpture, 1993

Stuart Caswell
Works on Paper, 1988

Francis M. Celentano
Painting, 1990

Enrique Chagoya-Flores
Works on Paper, 1992

Lauri Chambers
Painting, 1992

Frances Charteris
Photography, 1993

Susan Cheal
Painting, 1992

Tina Chinn
Crafts, 1993

Albert Chong
Photography, 1991

Charles B. Cobb
Crafts, 1989

Robert D. Cocke
Works on Paper, 1988

Tony Cockrell
Painting, 1992

Andrew S. Cooperman
Crafts, 1989

Dennis L. Cunningham
Works on Paper, 1988

Caryl Davis
Sculpture, 1991

Paul H. Davis
Works on Paper, 1988

Erik d'Azevedo
Painting, 1992

Roseline Delisle
Crafts, 1989

Susan Dunshee
Crafts, 1989

Tom Eckert
Crafts, 1989, 1993

C. C. Elian
Works on Paper, 1992

Dick Elliott
Sculpture, 1993

John O. Erickson
Painting, 1990

Judith Poxson Fawkes
Crafts, 1993

Alice Fellows
Painting, 1990

Lukas Felzmann
Photography, 1993

Mary Fish
Sculpture, 1993

Dan Fuller
Painting, 1990

Jeff Gambill
Painting, 1990

Terri Garland
Photography, 1991

Beth Lindsey Gellar
Sculpture, 1991

Cameron Gregg
Sculpture, 1991

Paul Harcharik
Works on Paper, 1992

Alfred Harris
Works on Paper, 1992

Lyle Ashton Harris
Photography, 1991

Thomas Harris
Photography, 1991

Randy Hayes
Works on Paper, 1988

Matt Heckert
Sculpture, 1991

F. Scott Hess
Painting, 1990

Caroline Lawson Hinkley
Photography, 1993

Anthony Holdsworth
Painting, 1990

David Hollowell
Works on Paper, 1988

Margaret Honda
Sculpture, 1991

Jody Isaacson
Works on Paper, 1988

Anne Griffin Johnson
Painting, 1990

Robert C. Jones
Painting, 1990

Kim Lee Kahn
Sculpture, 1991

Beanie Kaman
Works on Paper, 1992

Ed Kashi
Photography, 1991

Jeffrey C. Keith
Painting, 1990

Kimberly Kelzer
Crafts, 1993

Suzy Kerr
Photography, 1991

Young Kim
Photography, 1993

Don C. King
Crafts, 1989

Janine Klees
Sculpture, 1993

Cindy Kolodziejski
Crafts, 1993

Scott Kuykendall
Painting, 1990

Ann Lacy
Works on Paper, 1988

Gavin Lee
Photography, 1993

George Legrady
Photography, 1993

Leslie Lerner
Painting, 1990

Lauren Lesko
Sculpture, 1993

Carmalita Little Turtle
Photography, 1993

Jean Lowe
Sculpture, 1991, 1993

James Luna
Sculpture, 1991

Marilyn Lysohir
Crafts, 1989

Phyllis McGibbon
Works on Paper, 1992

Dianne Malley
Photography, 1991

Alden Mason
Painting, 1992

Myron J. Melnick
Crafts, 1989

Eric D. Nation
Crafts, 1993

John Neely
Crafts, 1989

Ronna Neuenschwander
Crafts, 1989

Heidi Oberheide
Painting, 1990

Brian O'Connor
Painting, 1990

Frank S. Okada
Painting, 1990

Mark C. Olsen
Photography, 1991

Ernie Pepion
Painting, 1992

Fran Reed
Crafts, 1993

David Regan
Crafts, 1993

Greg Reser
Painting, 1992

Glen Walter Rubsamen
Works on Paper, 1988

Ross Rudel
Sculpture, 1993

Yoshitomo Saito
Sculpture, 1993

Cristina Salvador
Photography, 1993

Stephen Schultz
Painting, 1990

June Schwarcz
Crafts, 1993

Robert Schwartz
Works on Paper, 1992

Vicki Scuri
Works on Paper, 1988

David A. Secrest
Crafts, 1989

Kathy Gaye Shiroki
Sculpture, 1991

Timothy Siciliano
Works on Paper, 1992

Paul Singdahlsen
Works on Paper, 1988

Christina Y. Smith
Crafts, 1989

Jaune Quick-To-See Smith
Works on Paper, 1988

Michael K. Speaker
Crafts, 1989

Linda A. Stark
Painting, 1992

George Stillman
Painting, 1990

Thaddeus Strode
Painting, 1992

Lynn Taber-Borcherdt
Painting, 1990

Brian D. Taylor
Photography, 1991

C. S. Tiefa
Works on Paper, 1988

Sarah M. Timberlake
Sculpture, 1991

Eric Van Eimeren
Crafts, 1993

Rudi Verhoeven
Painting, 1992

Christopher Warner
Painting, 1990

Gail Weissberg
Crafts, 1989

Albert J. Winn
Photography, 1993

Michele Zackheim
Works on Paper, 1988

INDEX and PHOTO CREDITS